Mountain Bike Maintenance

Mountain Bike Maintenance

Repairing and maintaining the off-road bicycle

Updated and expanded edition

Rob Van der Plas

Illustrated
by the author

Bicycle Books – San Francisco

Copyright	© Robert van der Plas, 1989, 1993 Second, fully updated and expanded edition, 1993
	Printed in the USA
Published by:	Bicycle Books, Inc. P.O. Box 2038 Mill Valley, CA 94941
Distributed to the book trade by:	USA: National Book Network, Lanham, MD Canada: Raincoast Book Distribution, Vancouver, BC
	UK: Chris Lloyd Sales & Marketing Services, Poole, Dorset
Cover photograph:	Neil van der Plas
Bicycle for cover photograph:	Gary Fisher Bicycles
Clothing for cover photograph:	A Bicycle Odyssey, Sausalito, CA

About the Author

Rob van der Plas is a professional engineer and a lifelong cyclist who has written about the subject for specialized magazines since 1975. In 1984, when the modern mountain bike was still in its prime, his *Mountain Bike Book*, the first book on the subject, was published. Since then, several other books by him were published by Bicycle Books, including *The Bicycle Repair Book, The Bicycle Touring Manual, The Bicycle Racing Guide* and *Bicycle Technology*.

Although many of the technical aspects are covered in some detail in the *Mountain Bike Book*, and repair instructions are available in some of his other books, it soon became obvious that there was a demand for a specialized handbook that covers specific repair and maintenance work as it applies to the mountain bike in exacting detail. That is the purpose of the present book.

Since the book's introduction, the mountain bike and its components had undergone so much evolution that a thorough review became necessary. This is the outcome: fully up-to-date, including attention to the latest developments in drivetrains, braking, gearing and accessories, the current edition of *Mountain Bike Maintenance* reflects the state of the art.

Author's Preface

This book is intended purely as a practical guide for repair and maintenance work on the modern mountain bike. If you are looking for information about riding and handling the bike, or for anecdotes and historical sketches about this wonderful machine and the people who developed it, you bought the wrong book.

But within the narrowly defined scope of a repair manual, I have made every effort to include all the information that seems relevant. Even so, there may be some instances of subjects not covered as thoroughly as some readers may desire. Or one reader or the other may know of better ways to tackle certain jobs. In either case, I would appreciate hearing from you.

Send any comments you may have to the author, care of Bicycle Books, Inc. (see copyright page for the mailing address). Any comments that merit inclusion will be incorporated in subsequent editions of the book.

Table of Contents

1. Know Your Mountain Bike . . . 11

About This Book 11
Terminology 11
The Parts of the Mountain Bike 12

2. The Tools for the Job 16

Selecting Tools 16
Universal Tools 17
Special Bicycle Tools 19
Lubricants and Cleaning Aids 21
Tools to Take Along 21
Additional Items 22
Spare Parts 23

3. Working on the Bike 24

Threaded Connections 24
Bowden Cables 26
Quick-Releases 28
Ball Bearings 28
Workshop and Bike Support 30
Buying Replacements and Tools 31
Preventive Maintenance 31
Daily Inspection 31
Bi-Weekly Inspection 32
Semi-Annual Inspection 33
Cleaning the Bike 34

4. The Frame 36

Frame Construction 36
Frame Damage 37
Frame Alignment Check 38
Rear Triangle Alignment 38
Drop-Out Check 39
Aligning Rear Drop-outs 40
Touching up Paint Damage 41

5. The Steering System 42

Handlebars and Stem 42
Adjusting or Tightening Handlebars 43
Tightening Handlebars in Stem 44
Replacing Handlebars with Stem 44
Replacing Handlebars or Stem 45
Shortening Handlebars 46
Replacing Handgrips 46
Bar Ends 47
The Headset 47
Adjusting Headset 47
Overhauling Headset 48
The Front Fork 49
Front Fork Inspection 50

Replacing Front Fork 50
Special Headsets 51
Suspension 51

**6. Saddle and
Seatpost** **52**

Adjusting Saddle Height 52
Adjusting Saddle Angle and Position . . . 53
Replacing Saddle with Seatpost 54
Replacing Seatpost or Saddle 54
Maintenance of Leather Saddle 55
Installing Sprung Leather Saddle 55

7. The Wheels . . . **57**

Replacing Wheel With Quick-Release . . . 57
Replacing Wheel with Axle Nuts 59
The Hub 60
Hub Bearing Check 61
Adjusting Hub Bearings 61
Lubricating Hub Bearing 62
Overhauling Hub 62
Rim and Spokes 63
Wheel Truing Check 64
Emergency Repair of Buckled Wheel 64
Wheel Truing 64
Replacing Spokes 65
Emergency Spoke Installation 66
Tire and Tube 66
Puncture Repair 67
Replacing Tube 71
Replacing Tire Casing 71
Patching Tire Casing 71

8. The Drivetrain . . **73**

The Bottom Bracket 73
Adjusting BSA Bottom Bracket 73
Overhauling Bottom Bracket 74
The Cranks 75
Replacing Crank 76
The Chainrings 77
Chainring Wear and Damage 78
Chainring Replacement 78
The Pedals 78
Replacing Pedal 79
Adjusting Pedal 79
Overhauling Regular Pedal 80
Clipless Pedals 81
The Chain 81
Replacing Chain 82
The Freewheel 84

Freewheel Lubrication 84
Freewheel Replacement 85
Replacing Screwed-On Freewheel 85
Replacing cassette Freewheel 86
Replacing Sprocket of Cassette Freewheel . 87
Replacing Sprocket of Screwed-On
    Freewheel 88
New Drivetrain Developments 88

9. The Gearing
System 89   System Overview 89
Adjusting Derailleur Range 90
The Rear Derailleur 91
Adjusting Rear Derailleur 92
Overhauling Rear Derailleur 94
Replacing Rear Derailleur 94
The Front Derailleur 95
Adjusting Front Derailleur 95
Replacing Front Derailleur 96
The Shifters 97
Replacing Shifter 97
Gear Cable 98
Replacing Derailleur Cable 98
New Developments 99

10. The Brakes . . 100   Brake Types 100
General Brake Check 101
Adjusting or Replacing Brake Pads 102
Adjusting Brake 102
Centering Cantilever Brake 103
Centering U-Brake 103
Roller-Cam Brake 104
Adjusting Roller-Cam Brake 104
Brake Overhauling or Replacement . . . 106
Adjusting Brake Lever 109
Adjusting Brake Cable 111
Replacing Brake Cable 112

11. Accessories . 114   The Lock 114
Lock Installation 114
Lock Maintenance 115
The Pump 115
Pump Maintenance 115
Seat Adjuster (Hite-Rite) 116
Replacing or Installing Hite-Rite 116
Toeclips 117
Lights 117

Installing Lights 118
Light Maintenance 118
Luggage Racks 119
Luggage Rack Installation 119
Fenders 119
Installing Fenders 120
Chainring Protector (Rockring) 120
Other Accessories 120
Accessory Installation and Maintenance . 121

Back Matter . . . **122** Troubleshooting Guide 122
Index 126
Other Books 128

Chapter 1
Know Your Mountain Bike

The present book is intended to help you keep your mountain bike in optimal condition. Nothing more, nothing less. You will find neither interesting detours into esoteric mountain biking cults, nor guidelines for riding techniques or equipment selection. But within the narrow range defined by the title, this book will give you essentially all the information you ever need to keep the mountain bike in optimal condition

About This Book

The approach of the book is simple: define the problem and show what to do about it. I will go about it as systematically as possible, first explaining what can be the cause of a specific problem, then proceeding with a list of required tools — or ways to substitute for the right tools, if they can't be rounded up — and finally step-by-step instructions for alleviating the problem. All that with simple and clear illustrations. Dull, but immensely practical. This edition includes advice on the latest products introduced.

Only the mountain bike and its technical peculiarities will be treated here. For those with other kinds of bikes, my *Bicycle Repair Book* will be useful. Here, you will find neither instructions on fixing a sew-up, or tubular tire, nor advice on adjusting racing handlebars or racing brakes, nor, at the other extreme, details of three-speed hubs and coaster brakes. Enough mountain bikes are sold these days to justify a book that specifically addresses their problems — and that more thoroughly than would be possible in the context of a more general bicycle repair book.

Terminology

As most of my works published by Bicycle Books, this same book will be sold in Britain and in the U.S. And as always, there will be cases of different names for the same thing in the two cultures. Aided by ten years exposure to each of these societies, I have made every effort to anticipate any such cases, though in general, I will be following US spelling conventions. Thus, tire will stand for tyre, center for centre, and aluminum for aluminium.

Of course, the difference between British and American English often goes well beyond spelling alone: braces become suspenders and spanners become wrenches as they travel from east to west across the Atlantic, to give but a few examples. Wherever relevant, I shall explain any different US terms, so others will understand what I am talking about. And wherever the text remains unclear, I am offering a free copy of the next (revised) edition of the book to the person who first points it out to me (care of Bicycle Books, Inc. — see the copyright page for address).

Finally, I should point out that I have little tolerance for some of the curious fruits of sexual emancipation as reflected in the use of language in presumably liberated circles. I consider compounds with -*person* equally unbearable as *he/she* and *him/her* expressions. Though I will try to avoid any terms that seem to exclude the female sex, there are cases where it is just not possible without getting involved in the kind of linguistic abominations that make it merely hard to read. I apologize if this offends anybody, but it is done with the best of intentions.

The Parts of the Mountain Bike

To do any work on the mountain bike, it is necessary to first know just what we are talking about and what the various components of the machine are called. Referring to Fig. 1.1, I shall now briefly describe the mountain bike and its major components. This is most easily done by taking the various functional groups of components one by one. That is the same way the various repair operations will be treated in individual chapters in the remaining parts of the book. The following functional groups may be distinguished:

☐   The frame

☐   The steering system

☐ Saddle and seatpost

☐ The wheels

☐ The drivetrain

☐ The gearing system

☐ The brakes

☐ Accessories

☐ Suspension.

The frame   The frame is covered in Chapter 4. It forms the backbone of the bicycle, on which the other components are installed by the manufacturer. It comprises the thick tubes of the main frame (head tube, top tube, down tube and seat tube), as well as the pairs of thinner tubes that make up the rear triangle: seat stays and chain stays. In addition, there is a bottom bracket, at the point where down tube, seat tube and chain stays meet, and various smaller parts. Fortunately, the frame rarely needs repair work. And if it does get damaged, it's usually time to get a new bike.

The steering system   The steering system, which is analyzed in Chapter 5, comprises the parts that allow balancing and steering the bike. These include the front fork, the handlebars, the stem that

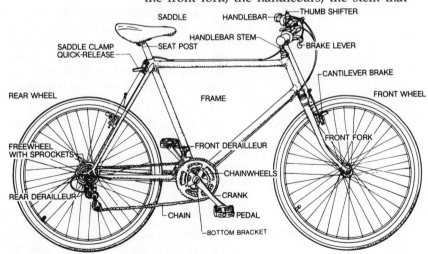

1.1 Parts of the mountain bike

attaches the handlebars to the fork, and the headset bearings that allow the steering system to pivot relative to the rest of the bike when the handlebars are turned.

The saddle
: The saddle is attached to the frame by means of the seatpost, which is clamped in the frame's seat tube by means of a quick-release binder bolt. Sometimes a spring-loaded height adjusting aid is supplied as well. All problems associated with the saddle are explained in Chapter 6.

The wheels
: The wheels, covered in Chapter 7, have thick knobby tires, enclosing an inner tube, both mounted on an aluminum rim that is held to the hub by means of thin spokes hooked into the central hub and screwed into nipples at the rim. The hub is either held to the frame and the fork with nuts threaded onto the axle or with a quick-release mechanism.

The drivetrain
: The drivetrain comprises the parts that transmit the rider's propulsive force to the rear wheel. As described in Chapter 8, it consists of the crankset, installed in the frame's bottom bracket shell, the pedals, the chain, the chainrings and the freewheel block installed on the rear wheel hub.

The gearing system
: The gearing system, covered in Chapter 9, comprises the front and rear derailleurs, which move the chain from one combination of chainring and sprocket, or cog, to another, and the shift levers mounted on the handlebars, as well as flexible cables that connect each shifter with its derailleur.

The brakes
: The brakes are also controlled by means of flexible cables from levers mounted on the handlebars. Once you pull the brake lever, the brake itself stops the wheel by squeezing two brake pads, or blocks, against the sides of the wheel rim. The various types of brakes used on the mountain bike will be covered in Chapter 10.

Accessories
: Accessories are additional components that can be installed on the bicycle. The maintenance and/or installation of lock, pump, seat

adjuster, lighting equipment, racks (luggage carriers to my British readers), fenders (mudguards) and chainring guard will be covered in Chapter 11.

Suspension During the last few years, many manufacturers have introduced bikes with suspension systems. Most typically, this means either a sprung front fork or at a minimum, a sprung handlebar stem. The most sophisticated models, meanwhile, even have a rear suspension, for which the frame must be specially adapted.

Now that we have covered at least enough of the basic bicycle nomenclature to know what we are talking about, we shall in the next two chapters look at the basics of bicycle care, before returning to the individual component groups of the mountain bike in the chapters that follow.

Chapter 2
The Tools for the Job

This and the next chapter will be devoted to very general themes. First I'll survey the most important tools required to work on the bike. In Chapter 3 I'll proceed to explain such frequently encountered details as cable adjustment, threaded connections, quick-releases and ball bearings. That same chapter also gives some guidelines for general preventive maintenance, following a simple regular schedule.

Although it's possible to spend several thousand dollars on bicycle tools, I have found that at least 90% of all maintenance and repair work can be done with a very modest outfit. And of those tools, only a few are so essential that they should also be taken along on most bike trips on the road or the trail. These tools include both regular or universal tools that can be bought at any hardware store, and specific bicycle tools that are available only from well stocked bike shops (or specialized mail order outlets).

Selecting Tools

Quality counts when buying tools even more than when dealing with other products. I have found quite similar looking tools at prices that varied by a factor of three — and in my youthful ignorance I have only too often chosen the cheaper version. That's a mistake, because the tool that costs one third as much doesn't last even a third as long. Besides, it never fits as accurately, often leading to damage both of the part handled and the tool itself. After some unsatisfactory use, you'll probably decide to get the better tool anyway, so you finish up spending quite a bit more than you would have done buying the highest quality tool right away.

Having sworn to buy only the best tools for the job, we can now get down to a brief description of the various essential tools of both categories — universal tools and special bicycle tools. Even more uncommon items, that are used only rarely if at all by the amateur bike mechanic, will be described in the chapters where their application becomes relevant.

Below, you will find most of the common tools described, some — though not all — of them with an illustration. Don't be discouraged by the length of the list, since you don't really need every one of the items described here. Refer to the section on *Tools to Take Along* for the really essential tools that should be bought right away.

All the other tools can wait until you have a specific need. Most bicycle components are built with metric threading, and thus metric tool sizes will be required. The size quoted in mm (millimeters) will be the dimension across flats of the point where the tool fits — not the size of the screw thread, as is customary for American and Whitworth sizes.

Universal Tools

These are the basic tools that can be purchased in any hardware shop. I will point out which sizes are appropriate for mountain bike maintenance jobs.

Screwdriver The screwdriver's size is designated by the blade width at the end. You will need a small one with a 4 mm (3⁄16 in.) blade, a larger one with a 6–7 mm (1⁄4"–5⁄32 in.) blade, and perhaps a Phillips type if your bike has any screws with cross-shaped recesses instead of the conventional saw cut.

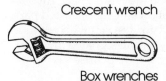

SCREWDRIVER

REGULAR BLADE   PHILLIPS HEAD BLADE

Crescent wrench This is an adjustable wrench, designated by its overall length. Get a 150 mm (6 in.) long model and one that is at least 200 mm (8 in.), preferably even 250 mm (10 in.) long.

Box wrenches These are the most accurate tools for tightening or loosening nuts and bolts with hexagonal heads. Like all other fixed wrenches, they are designated by the across-flats dimension of the bolt on which they fit, always measured in mm. You will need sizes from 7 mm to 16 mm.

Open-ended wrenches These are the most common wrenches available. They can be used when there is not

enough access room for the box wrench. Get a set in sizes from 7 mm to 16 mm.

Combination wrench

This type has a box wrench on one end and an open-ended wrench of the same size on the other. Even better than a set each of the preceding items, is to get two sets of these, again in sizes from 7 mm to 16 mm.

Allen keys

These hexagonal L-shaped bars are used on the screws with hexagonal recesses often used on mountain bikes. They are designated by the across-flats dimension and you will probably just need these in the sizes 2, 4 mm, 5 mm and 6 mm.

Pliers

The three models illustrated may find a use occasionally, but I suggest you don't get tempted to use any one of them whenever another better fitting tool will do the job, since pliers often do more damage than necessary.

Hammers

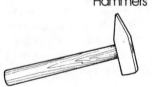

These are classified by their weight. I suggest a 300 gram (10 oz.) metal working model, which has a square head at one end and a wedge-shaped one on the other. In addition, you may need a mallet with a plastic head of about the same weight.

Hacksaw

When all else fails, you may find a need for one of these, e.g. to remove a tangled or rusted part or to provide a hold for the screwdriver in a damaged bolt. They are designated by their blade length. I find the 8-in. Eclipse saw quite adequate.

Files

These are designated by the length of their blade and their coarseness. For bicycle use, get a relatively fine 8-in. file to remove the occasional protruding spoke or a burr at the end of a part that is cut off or damaged.

Provisional tools

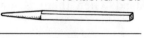

These include some simple metal-working tools, like punch, drift and cold chisel, that may be needed to tighten or loosen specific parts of

the bike when no fitting tool is at hand. The cold chisel should be ground blunt, since you will not use it for its original purpose of cutting metal, but rather to unscrew a part with notches.

Special Bicycle Tools

The following list of tools made specifically for bicycle use includes almost all the tools you will be likely to need as a home mechanic. A much more modest selection — those listed under *Tools to Take Along* — will usually get you by when no really major operations have to be carried out.

Even more special tools will be mentioned as we get into the actual maintenance instructions. In many cases, you will have to consult the bike shop to make sure you get the size or model of any particular tool that matches the parts installed on your bike. For that reason, it is best to have the bike with you whenever buying tools.

Pump Although often considered an accessory rather than a tool, it's also an essential tool, especially on the mountain bike, since you may be riding the bike far from the nearest gas station or garage. Make sure you get a model that matches the particular valves used on your bike (Presta or Schrader, as described in Chapter 7). See Chapter 11 for maintenance. A CO_2 inflator will speed up the process, but each full tire inflation may require a new cartridge, so it's not much use except when you are racing.

head

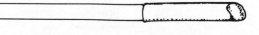

Pressure gauge In addition to the pump, I suggest you invest in a pressure gauge to make sure you inflate the tires correctly, at least to use at home — again matching the valve used on your bicycle's tires.

Tire levers Still referred to as tire irons in some circles in the US, these are now usually made of plastic. They are used to lift the tire off the rim in case of a flat (puncture) or when replacing tube or tire. Most mountain bike tires fit loosely enough on the rim to use only one or two, and

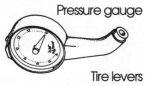

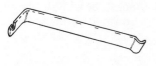

some can actually be removed without. You should select thin, flat ones that don't bend.

Tire repair kit   Contains most of the other essentials for fixing a flat: patches, rubber solution, sandpaper. This little box also comes in handy to carry some other small spare parts, such as extra nuts and bolts, pump washer, light bulbs and the like.

Spoke wrench   Called nipple spanner in Britain, it is used to tighten, remove or install a spoke, either to replace it or in order to straighten a bent wheel. Make sure you get one that has at least one cut-out in the size that matches the spoke nipples used on your bike.

Crank extractor   Illustrated on page 64, this tool is needed to tighten or loosen the cranks. Make sure you get a model that matches the cranks installed on your bike, since they vary from make to make, sometimes even from model to model.

Freewheel extractor   Used to remove a freewheel block from the rear hub, which may be necessary to replace something as basic as a broken spoke. This tool must also be selected to match the particular freewheel used on your bike.

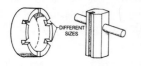

Chain whip   This device is used to remove individual sprockets from the freewheel. Depending on the kind of freewheel on the bike, you may either need two or one in conjunction with the manufacturer's special wrench, as outlined in Chapter 9.

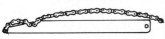

Chain rivet tool   Illustrated in Chapter 10, this tool is used to remove a pin that connects the links of the (endless) chain, so it can be separated for maintenance.

Cone wrenches (spanners)   These very flat open-ended wrenches are used to overhaul the bearings of a wheel hub. Available in several sizes — get two of each of the sizes needed for the hubs on your bike.

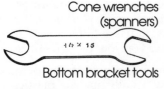

Bottom bracket tools   Needed for maintenance operation on the crankset or bottom bracket bearings. Many mountain bikes are equipped with bottom brackets that need quite specific tools for this

work, so make sure to match the tools to the components on your bike.

Headset tools These are oversize flat open-ended wrenches, used to overhaul the steering system's headset bearings. Since the introduction of OS (oversize) headsets, their size and shape also vary as discussed in Chapter 5.

Lubricants and Cleaning Aids

In addition to the tools listed above, you will need some materials to help you clean the bike and its parts and to lubricate for minimal friction and maximum durability. Use the following items:

Rags You'll need at least one clean, one greasy rag. The latter is made that way by applying either vaseline or bearing grease.

Brushes Get two sizes, about 20 mm (¾ in.) and 40 mm (1½ in.) wide, respectively.

Solvent Use either turpentine, kerosene or an other solvent.

Bearing grease Either the special kind sold under the brand name of some bicycle component manufacturer or any regular lithium-based bearing grease.

Oil You can use e.g. SAE 40 motor oil or SAE 60 gear oil.

Containers A flat container to catch drippings or to clean parts in.

Penetrating oil A spraycan of thin, penetrating lubricant, such as WD-40.

Chain lube A spraycan of special chain lubricant.

Wax Used to protect bare metal parts, any car wax will serve the purpose.

Cleaning aids Many cleaning jobs are done simply with a rag and water, while some items may have to be cleaned with a mixture of solvent with about 5–10% mineral oil.

Tools to Take Along

Only a very limited selection of the tools listed above are so essential that you should carry them along on your rides. On the mountain bike, you should probably be more generous in

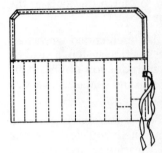

what to take along than you might be when riding on paved roads in built-up areas, since there is not much chance of getting help on the way, let alone hitching a ride home or to the nearest gas station. The following is just my personal preference. In addition to that, refer to the section on spare parts below for other items that should be carried.

After you have had some experience, you may decide to expand or modify this list to include the items *you* are most comfortable with. Carry them in a bag tied to the bike (e.g. a saddle bag — select a bag that does not dangle freely: it should be strapped to the seatpost and the saddle). Alternately, you can make a pouch as illustrated, carried either in a bike bag or tied directly to a frame tube or under the saddle. Here's what I suggest taking along:

☐   pump (for mountain bike racing, use a CO_2 inflator instead, to save time

☐   4 mm screwdriver

☐   2 tire levers (unless your tire fits loosely enough to remove the tire by hand)

☐   tire patch kit

☐   6-in. adjustable wrench

☐   7—14 mm open-ended or box wrenches

☐   2, 4, 5, 6 mm Allen keys

☐   needle-nose pliers

☐   spoke wrench

☐   chain rivet tool

☐   crank extractor.

Additional Items

In addition — depending on the length and the purpose of the trip —, you may want to carry some of the spares listed in the next section. Equally important are the following items: a bottle of water installed on the bike, a tube of waterless hand cleaner, a rag or tissues, and a small first aid kit, including a pair of scissors and a pocket knife, and perhaps some lubricant in a spray can or a well sealed bottle. Finally, carry a lock, in case you have to leave the bike behind while getting help.

Spare Parts

Here is a list of the spare parts you may find useful to carry on a longer trip. Usually, I get by admirably well without many of these. Only twice in 40 years and 200 000 miles of cycling, have I not been able to patch a punctured tube and found I really needed a spare tube. But a lot depends on the conditions of the trip: in mountain bike racing, or even when you are out with a larger group, it's essential to get back on the bike as quickly as possible, making it more sensible to replace rather than patch. On the other hand, you may well get two or more punctures on one trip, so it will be smarter to at least have the tools to fix the problem when your spares are depleted.

At the other extreme, many people seem to feel you can't have too many spares. My feeling is that adequate preventive maintenance will forestall almost all repairs that require an extensive spare parts inventory. With all that in mind, be guided by the following list:

- ☐ Brake cable (inner cable only, long enough for rear brake).
- ☐ Derailleur cable (inner cable only, long enough for rear derailleur).
- ☐ Spokes with matching nipples, making sure they are of the right length for both wheels.
- ☐ Hooked emergency spokes as described in Chapter 7 for the RH side of the rear wheel.
- ☐ Bolts, washers, and nuts in 4, 5 and 6 mm sizes.
- ☐ Grommet (rubber seal washer) for pump.
- ☐ If you will be riding in the dark, light bulbs and batteries for front and rear light.
- ☐ Inner tube.

Chapter 3
Working on the Bike

Before proceeding to more detailed repair and maintenance instructions for particular systems and components of the bike and specific problems, the first part of this chapter will be devoted to the techniques for handling some basic mechanisms found in many places on your mountain bike. This includes screw-threaded connections in general, cables and their adjustment, as well as ball bearings and their adjustment and lubrication. The second part of this chapter will be devoted to preventive maintenance.

Threaded Connections

Many of the bicycle's parts are attached, installed and themselves constructed with threaded connections — not only nuts and bolts, but many other components as well. Essentially, all threaded connections are based on the same principle: a cylindrical, male, part is threaded into a corresponding hollow, female, part by means of matching helical grooves cut into each. When the one part is threaded fully into the other, the reaction force pushes the sides of male and female threads against one another, creating so much friction that the parts are no longer free to turn, thus keeping the connection firm.

3.1 Screw thread details

Fig. 3.1 shows the details of a typical threaded connection, including an enlarged detail of a cross section through the thread. Screw threads are designated by their nominal size, generally measured in mm in the bicycle industry. In addition, the pitch, or number of threads per inch, and the thread angle may vary, and finally some parts have LH (left hand) threading, instead of the regular RH (right hand) thread. LH thread is found on the LH pedal, as well as on a few bearing parts of the mountain bike.

Regular nuts and bolts are standardized — for a given nominal diameter, they will have the same pitch and the same thread angle, and they all have RH thread. Many other bicycle com-

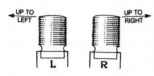

3.2 LH and RH screw thread

ponents are less standardized: there are at least three different industry standards for such parts as headsets, bottom brackets and freewheels. Though mountain bikes are virtually all built to the BCI (British Cycle Institute) standard dimensions, chances are you buy a component some day that turns out to have e.g. French or Italian threading. To avoid such mismatching, always take the part to be replaced, as well as a matching component to which it is threaded, to the bike store when buying a replacement, so you can try it out there.

Whether we are talking about a regular nut and bolt or any other threaded part, the way to loosen and tighten the connection is the same. The one part has to be restrained, while the other is turned relative to it — to the right to tighten, the left to loosen in the case of RH thread, the other way round for LH thread. Fig. 3.2 shows how to tell them apart if they are not marked. Use exactly fitting tools, to give the best possible hold and to minimize damage. Use tools that offer some leverage (e.g. a wrench with a long handle) on the part that is turned, while the part that is merely restrained may be held with less leverage (e.g. a screwdriver or a shorter wrench).

3.3 Screw thread locking devices

All threaded connections should be clean and lightly greased when they are installed. If you have difficulty loosening a connection, first squirt some penetrating oil, such as WD-40, at any accessible point where the male part disappears in the female part. To allow a nut or the head of a bolt to be turned when it is hard down on the part it holds, a plain washer should be installed between the two. This allows you to tighten the joint more firmly.

To minimize the chances of coming loose, e.g. on account of vibrations while riding, many threaded connections are secured one way or another. Fig. 3.3 shows a number of methods used to achieve this: locknut, spring washer and locking insert nut. The locknut is a second nut that is tightened against the main nut, creating high friction forces in the threads working opposite ways. The spring washer expands to hold the connection when vibration would otherwise loosen it, and the locking insert nut has a nylon insert that is deformed by the threading, offering the required high resistance against loosening. If you have problems with parts coming loose, you may use any of these techniques to secure them. A connection that comes loose frequently despite such locking device is probably worn to the point where replacement — usually of both parts — is in order.

Bowden Cables

Brakes and gears on the mountain bike are operated via flexible Bowden cables that connect the brake or shift lever with the main unit. Fig. 3.4 shows details of a typical cable, while Fig. 3.5 illustrates the pertinent adjusting mechanism. The inner cable takes up tension forces, which are countered by the compression forces taken up by the casing, or outer cable. To minimize the resistance of the inner cable running in the casing, the later's length is minimized by having part of the inner cable run free between stops that are mounted on the bike's frame.

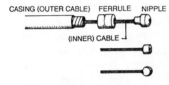

CASING (OUTER CABLE)   FERRULE   NIPPLE

(INNER) CABLE

3.4 Bowden cable details

A nipple is soldered on at one end of the inner cable, while the other end is clamped in at the brake or gear mechanism. Ferrules are installed at the ends of the cable casing to provide a firm termination at the anchor points. There will be several different cables on your bike, and you should take care to get the right kind. In addition to the different nipple shapes in use by different makers to match particular components, the thickness can vary. Usually an end cap is crimped (i.e. squeezed) around the free end of the inner cable — pull it off with pliers when replacing the cable.

The cables for index gearing controls are designed to be rather stiff so they can take up some compressive, as well as tensile, forces. The inner cables for brake controls must be quite thick to take up the high forces without stretching. Make sure the outer cable has the right diameter for the pertinent inner cable to slide through freely.

The cables for the brakes and the one for the front derailleur should be cleaned and lubricated regularly, while the one for the rear derailleur should only be kept clean, without lubrication. This assumes your bike is equipped with an indexed rear derailleur, as virtually all mountain bikes sold since 1987 are.

The index system invariably uses a stainless steel inner cable with a nylon sleeve between it and the inside of the casing, which makes lubrication unnecessary. By way of lubrication for a regular cable, you may put some grease or vaseline on a rag and run this rag over the inner cable. Once the cable is installed, you may use spraycan lubricant, aiming with the nozzle at the points where the inner cable disappears into the outer casing. Remove excess lubricant with a rag to keep things clean.

When replacing cables, I suggest using stainless steel inner cables, making sure you select them with the same shape nipple used on the original. Some cable casings are available with a low-friction liner of either nylon or PTFE; these eliminate a lot of potential maintenance problems.

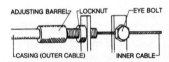

3.5 Adjusting detail

Adjusting the cable tension is often necessary to adjust brakes or gears. To this purpose, an adjusting mechanism as shown in Fig. 3.5 is generally installed somewhere along the length of the cable. Before attempting adjustment, make sure the cable end is clamped in firmly. To adjust, loosen the lock nut (usually a round knurled design), while restraining the adjusting barrel. Next, unscrew the adjusting barrel far enough to obtain the desired cable tension, and finally tighten the locknut while holding the adjusting barrel to restrain it.

If the length of the adjusting barrel does not allow enough adjusting range, the inner cable must be clamped in further. To do this, first back up the locknut all the way while restraining the adjusting barrel, then screw the adjusting barrel in all the way, and finally clamp the cable in a new location, while keeping it pulled taut with the aid of a pair of pliers.

Quick-Releases

Quick-release mechanisms are used on the seat clamp and often on the wheels, while some brake levers also come equipped with some mechanism to untension the brake quickly. The quick-releases for saddle clamp and wheel hubs work on the same principle. Instead of holding the axle or bolt by means of one or two nuts that are screwed down, a toggle lever is used, as shown in Fig. 3.6.

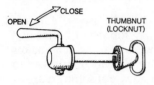

3.6 Quick-release operation

The thumbnut is not intended to be used for tightening the connection, but merely to adjust it in such a way that twisting the lever tightens the whole connection firmly. Open the lever by twisting it, close it by twisting it back. If the connection does not hold, first place the lever in the open position, then tighten the thumbnut perhaps half a turn and try again, until the lever not only holds the part firmly, but can also be opened enough to allow removal or adjustment of the part in question.

Ball Bearings

There are at least 14 sets of ball bearing in every mountain bike: two each in the hubs, the headset, the pedals, the bottom bracket and the freewheel. They all work on the same principle and their condition has a great effect on the bike's performance. Understanding their operation, maintenance and adjustment is as important for every home bike mechanic as it is for the occasional cyclist who just wants to be sure his bike is operating optimally.

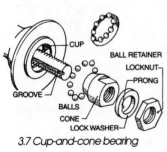

3.7 Cup-and-cone bearing

Two kinds of bearings are in use: cup-and-cone, or adjustable, bearings as shown in Fig. 3.7, and cartridge bearings (often referred to as sealed bearings) as shown in Fig. 3.8. Though the latter are generally more accurate when new and can be better sealed against dirt and water, they are not inherently superior. Besides, there is little maintenance you can do on these models: either they run smoothly or they must be replaced, which is best to leave to a bike mechanic, since it generally requires special tools. Sometimes — but not usually — subsequent lubrication is allowed for by means of an oil hole or a grease nipple that is integrated in the part in which the bearings are installed. In other cases, the best you can do is to lift off the seal with a pointed object and apply grease.

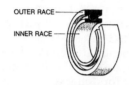

3.8 Cartridge bearing details

The more common cup-and-cone bearing consists of a cone-shaped and a cup-shaped bearing race, one of which is adjustable relative to the other by means of screw threading. The bearing balls lie in the recess between these two parts and are lubricated to minimize friction. Generally, bearing grease is used as a lubricant. Actually, oil — any thickish mineral oil — is even more effective, but tends to be messy.

To lubricate with oil, there must be an oil hole in the part. Use an oil can with a narrow spout. Put a shallow receptacle under the part to be lubricated and fill oil into the oil hole until it comes out the other end, then allow it to drip a few minutes and wipe it clean with a rag. Repeat at least once a month and after every ride in very dusty or wet terrain.

Grease lubrication only has to be repacked once a season. But to do it, you have to disassemble the entire bearing, as explained in the relevant chapters. Clean and inspect all parts, replacing anything that appears to be damaged (corroded, pitted or grooved). Then fill the cup-shaped bearing race with bearing grease and push the bearing balls in, leaving enough space to allow their free movement, followed by reassembly and subsequent adjustment. The bearing balls are often held in a retainer, and when overhauling a sticky bearing, it may be wise to replace that by loose balls, often resulting in at least temporary relief.

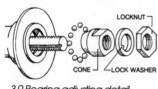

3.9 Bearing adjusting detail

Adjustable bearings must be so adjusted that the moving part is free to rotate with minimal friction, yet has no 'play' (looseness). To adjust a cup-and-cone bearing, loosen the locknut or lockring while holding the underlying part (the cone in the case of a hub or a pedal, the cup in the case of a headset or bottom bracket). Next, lift the underlying lock washer, if installed, and tighten or loosen the threaded main bearing part (cone or cup) about a quarter of a turn at a time. Finally hold that part again, while tightening the locknut or lockring. Repeat the whole operation if necessary.

Workshop and Bike Support

When you are out in terrain or on the road, you can't be too picky, but when doing maintenance or repair work at home, I recommend you provide a minimum of organized workshop space. It needn't be a separate room, nor must it be a permanently designated location. But while working on the bike, it should be adequately equipped for doing so.

3.10 Bike repair stand

The amount of space needed is quite modest: 2.10 m x 1.8 m (7 ft. x 6 ft.) is enough for any maintenance work ever done on the bike. As a minimum, you should equip this area with the tools and the cleaning and lubrication aids listed in the preceding chapter. In addition, you will need a workbench — although the kitchen counter or an old table will do. Ideally, you should install a sizable metalworking vice on the workbench, although probably 98% of all the jobs described in this book can be carried out without.

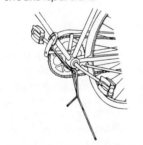

3.11 Display stand as support

Next, you will want a support for the bike. The best ones are freestanding devices or those mounted against the wall. I suggest you buy a contraption like the one shown in Fig. 3.10 to support the bike off the ground. A simple but adequate alternative is a metal-wire bike display stand placed under the bottom bracket. Another solution is to turn the bike upside down, supporting it at the handlebars by means of the home-made device shown in Fig. 3.12. It serves to raise the handlebars off the ground far enough to protect anything mounted there.

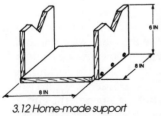

3.12 Home-made support

Unlike the racing bike with its dropped handlebars, the mountain bike can usually be placed upside down without such a support reasonably well, merely turning the shifters out of the way to protect them, and that is what you will have to do when you have a problem while far from home. Just don't forget to do just that each time you turn it over without adequate support, using a screwdriver to loosen the clamps that attach the shifters — and tightening them again in the proper position when you have finished.

Buying Replacements and Tools

Whenever you have to buy a replacement part for the bike, it is best to take either the whole bike or at least the old part and one matching component (e.g. the nut as well as the bolt, the handlebars as well as the stem, when replacing either one) to the store with you to make sure to get perfectly matching components. The same goes for buying tools for specific jobs, because many makes and models of superficially similar parts exist, each requiring a perfect fit.

Preventive Maintenance

At the risk of being trite, I must emphasize that in bicycle maintenance, an ounce of prevention is worth a pound of repairs. It is actually very simple to keep the bike in good operating condition, so it is working well whenever you ride it. That will eliminate the vast majority of necessary repairs later on. It's all a matter of knowing what to look for and how to put it right before it becomes serious. It will be easy enough to spot when a nut or a bearing has come loose, and if corrected immediately, no harm will be done. Yet left unchecked, the situation rapidly becomes worse, often leading to an expensive and complicated replacement job after only a week or so of neglect.

Though most of the actual maintenance operations are covered in detail in the chapters that follow, this is the time to get familiar with a systematic schedule to check the bike. It is based on (almost) daily, bi-weekly and bi-annual checks, proceeding as outlined below, referring to the individual chapters that follow to make any corrections that may be necessary.

Daily Inspection

That may seem to be overdoing it a little, but there are a few things you ought to look out for whenever you take the bike out. These will be covered in this section.

Tires   Check whether the tires are inflated properly, considering the type of terrain you will ride in: 4–5 bar (60–75 psi) for smooth, hard roads, 3 bar (45 psi) for rough but hard surfaces, 2 bar (30 psi) for irregular but mainly firm ground, 1 bar (15 psi) for really loose ground, ice or soft snow.

Handlebars   Make sure the handlebars are straight and at the right height.

Saddle   Verify that the saddle is straight and level and at the right height.

Brakes   Check the effectiveness of the brakes by verifying each can block the wheel against your weight pushing the bike forward with the lever depressed, leaving about two cm (¾ in.) between brake lever and handlebars.

Gears   Lift the rear wheel and, while turning the cranks, check whether the derailleurs can be shifted to reach all the gears — i.e. every combination of chainring and sprocket.

Bi-Weekly Inspection

At least every other week during the time you use the bike, clean it as explained below. Then carry out the same inspections listed above for the daily inspection, and in addition do the following:

Wheels   Check for broken spokes and wheel wobble: lift the wheel off the ground and turn it relatively slowly, keeping an eye on a fixed point such as the brake blocks. If the wheel seems to wobble sideways relative to the fixed point, it should be trued (see Chapter 7).

Brakes   Observe what happens when you pull the brake levers forcefully: the brake blocks must touch the side of the rim over their entire surface. Adjust the brake as outlined in Chapter 10 if they don't.

Tires   Check the tires for external damage and embedded objects. Remove anything that doesn't belong there and replace the tire if necessary.

Cranks   Using the wrench part of the crank extractor tool, pull the crank attachment bolts tight, as explained in Chapter 8.

General Inspection   Check all the other bolts and nuts to make sure they are tight, verify whether all moving parts turn freely and all adjustments are correct. Repair or replace anything damaged or missing.

Lubrication   Lubricate the parts shown in Fig. 3.13, using the lubricants indicated below and wiping any excess off again afterwards:

Chain: special chain lube in spraycan;

Brake levers, pivots, cable ends: light spraycan lubricant, aiming precisely with the little tubular nozzle installed on the spray head;

Exposed blank metal parts: car wax.

Semi-Annual Inspection

3.13 Lubrication points

Yes, twice a year — that's how often I think the work described below will be necessary, though once a year may be enough if you only ride in the summer. This is a complete overhauling job, which very nearly returns the bike to its as-bought condition. Treated this way, your mountain bike will literally last a lifetime, unless of course you have a collision that destroys the frame. But even then, on a high-quality bike, it may be worthwhile to salvage most of the parts, replacing only what was actually damaged.

If you only use the bike in the fair-weather period, carry out this work at the end of the season. Then merely carry out a bi-weekly inspection at the beginning of the next season. During the semi-annual inspection, proceed as follows:

First carry out all the work described above for the bi-weekly inspection, noting in particular which parts need special attention because they seem to be loose, worn, damaged or missing. Subsequently, work down the following list:

Wheels   With the wheels still installed, check for damage of the rim, the tire and missing spokes, then remove the wheels and overhaul the hubs, as described in Chapter 7, repacking them with bearing grease. This work is not necessary if you lubricate with oil or the hubs have cartridge bearings — as long as they are operating perfectly smoothly and without play.

Hubs   Check the hubs for play, wear and tightness as explained in Chapter 7. Preferably disassemble and lubricate or overhaul the hubs.

Chain   Remove the chain and measure the length of a 100 link section — replace the entire chain if it measures more than 51 in. (129.5 cm). The apparent stretch is a sign of wear that will affect shifting as well as transmission efficiency. In addition, the worn chain will also wear out the chainrings and the sprockets. If the chain is not badly worn, merely rinse it out in solvent, after which it should be lubricated immediately (to prevent rust) and reinstalled, following the instructions in Chapter 8.

Bottom bracket   Check it for play and freedom of rotation. If the bottom bracket is of the adjustable type, remove the crank and disassemble and overhaul the bearings as explained in Chapter 8. If it has cartridge bearings and does not run properly, get it overhauled at the bike shop

Headset   Try it out and make sure it rotates without play or rough spots. Preferably, disassemble and overhaul the bearings as described in Chapter 5

Derailleurs   With the chain removed, clean, check and lubricate both derailleur mechanisms, making sure the pivots work smoothly and the little wheels, or pulleys, of the rear derailleur turn freely. If necessary, overhaul or replace parts as explained in Chapter 9.

GreaseGuard Note   An excellent form of lubrication is that by means of the GreaseGuard fittings installed on some high-end SunTour and special hubs, bottom brackets and headsets. Here grease is squirted in at each bearing and trapped in place by means of a chevron-shaped seal.

Cleaning the Bike

Do this job whenever your bike gets dirty — at least once a month in clean terrain and dry weather, much more frequently in dirty terrain and bad weather.

Cleaning procedure

1.   If the bike is dry, wipe it with a soft brush or a rag to remove any dust and other dry dirt. If the bike — or the dirt that adheres to it — is wet, hose or sponge it down with plenty of clean water. Take care not to get the water into the hubs, bottom bracket and headset bearings, though. The same goes for a leather saddle.

2.   Using a damp cloth, clean in all the hard-to-get-at nooks and crannies. Wrap the rag around a pointed object, like a screwdriver, to get into hidden places, e.g. between the sprockets on the freewheel and the chainrings, underneath the brake arms, or at the derailleur pulleys.

3.   Clean and dry the same locations with a clean, soft, dry cloth.

4.   With a clean wax- or vaseline-soaked rag, treat all the blank metal areas very sparingly to inhibit rust.

5.   Once or twice a year, it may be worthwhile to apply car wax to the paintwork. Similarly, blank metal parts may have to be treated with chrome polish to remove traces of corrosion and erosion before applying wax.

Chapter 4
The Frame

Although the frame is the bicycle's major single part, it is fortunately rarely in need of maintenance or repair work. And when something does happen, it is likely to be so serious that the average rider decides to call it a day and perhaps even abandon the bike. Just the same, there are some maintenance aspects of the frame that will be covered here.

Frame Construction

Fig. 4.1 shows how the frame of your mountain bike is built up. The front part, or main frame, is made up of large diameter tubes, called top tube, down tube, seat tube and head tube, respectively. The bottom bracket shell is at its lowest point. The rear triangle is built up of double sets of smaller diameter tubes, called seat stays and chain stays, respectively. Each pair is connected by means of a short bridge piece.

Most mountain bikes are constructed by welding the tubes together. Some frames are built with fillet-brazed joints, where the tubes are brazed (silver- or bronze-soldered) together with smooth contours. Still other frames are built with lugs that connect the tubes of the main frame, just like most road bikes. Finally,

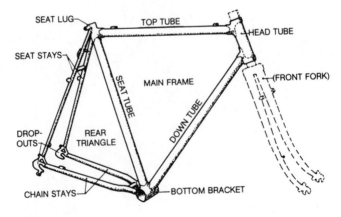

4.1 Parts of the frame

some frames of special materials may have bonded joints.

Whether welded, brazed or bonded, one lug is always present: the seat lug. It is split in the back and clamped together to hold the saddle. At the ends where the stays meet there are flat plates, called drop-outs, in which the wheels are installed. The one on the right also contains a threaded eye, in which the derailleur is mounted. Finally, there are a number of small parts, referred to as braze-ons. These range from the pivot bosses for the mountain bike's special brakes to little bosses for the installation of water bottle and luggage rack, cable guides, etc.

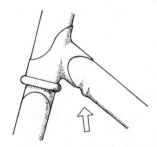

4.2 Down tube damage

Although most frames are made of some kind of steel tubing, quite a few mountain bike frames are made of aluminum — these are generally the frames with very large diameter tubes. Neither material is inherently superior to the other. In fact, aluminum frames are not necessarily lighter than steel frames, due to the larger tube diameters required for adequate strength and rigidity. Most aluminum frames are welded, while some are bonded together with the aid of internal or external lugs. Finally, there are composite frames made in part with resin-embedded fibers.

Frame Damage

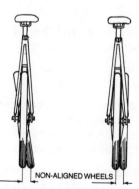

NON-ALIGNED WHEELS

4.3 Wheel misalignment

Mountain bike frames subjected to serious off-road cycling sometimes get damaged. In case of a head-on collision, there is a chance of the down tube literally buckling at a point just behind the head tube, as shown in Fig. 4.2. Left unchecked, this will eventually lead to the frame's collapse, which may prove highly dangerous. It's the kind of damage only a professional frame builder can solve for you and one that's only worthwhile on an expensive frame: the down tube has to be removed and replaced by a new one. After a serious head-on collision, check the appropriate location for damage. If it is buckled, take the bike to a bike shop to find out what can be done about it.

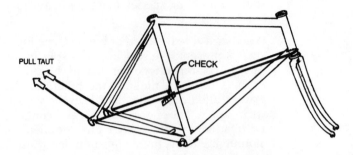

4.4 Frame alignment check

Other kinds of frame damage are less dramatic, though they may be serious enough. A collision, a fall or other forms of abuse may cause the frame to get out of alignment. You can verify this from time to time by trying to line up front and rear wheel as shown in Fig. 4.3 while looking from behind. If it can't be done, either the frame or the front fork is probably misaligned. The descriptions below show you how to check the frame and what to do about it. Finally, it sometimes happens that one of the drop-outs gets bent. Instructions to establish and correct this problem are also contained below.

Frame Alignment Check

In this and the following procedures, all the checks that can be carried out relatively simply will be described in some detail. Always see a bike shop about correcting any damage detected.

Tools and equipment:
3 m (10 ft.) of twine, ruler marked in mm or 32nds

Procedure:
1.   Remove the rear wheel from the bike, following the relevant description in Chapter 7.

2.   Wrap the twine around the frame as shown in Fig. 4.4, pulling it taut at the dropouts.

3.   Measure and compare the distance between seat tube and twine on both sides. If the difference is more than 3 mm (⅛ in.), the frame is out of alignment and should be corrected.

Rear Triangle Alignment

Occasionally, the misalignment is due to a minor deformation of the tubes of the rear triangle. If this is the case, you may be able to correct it yourself — at least on most steel frames (it can't be done on composite frames, and is not safe to do on aluminum, titanium and very light steel frames). Check the tubes of the rear triangle for serious and abrupt damage. If this is the case, get advice from a bike mechanic. If not, proceed with the correction procedure described here, repeating the preceding check as you proceed, to verify you don't make the situation worse.

Tools and equipment:
none required, but two people needed to carry out the work

Procedure:
1.   Place the frame on a solid raised surface, such as a work bench, as shown in Fig. 4.5. The side of the rear triangle that has to be bent out (as established in the preceding check) facing down, or the part that has to be bent in facing up.

2.   One person stands on the main frame at seat tube and head tube.

3.   The other person carefully forces the rear triangle in the required direction.

4.   Check frame alignment and repeat the operation until you are satisfied.

Note: Though this kind of work can be done quite satisfactorily, it is generally preferable to consult an experienced bike mechanic and have him or her do the work for you.

Drop-Out Check

After a fall, the reason for derailleur problems may be that the rear derailleur eye (on the RH rear drop-out) is bent. In other cases, the wheel doesn't seem to center, even though it seems to be undamaged (as checked in Chapter 7). To establish whether the drop-outs are still straight after a fall or rough transportation — this damage is more typically caused by the latter — proceed as follows:

Tools and equipment:
60 cm (2 ft.) long metal straightedge

Procedure:
1.   Remove the rear wheel from the bike, following the relevant procedure in Chapter 7.

2.   Hold the straightedge snug up against the outside of the RH drop-out, holding, but not forcing, the other end near the down tube and measure the distance between the straightedge and the seat tube.

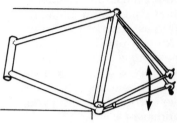

4.5 Rear triangle straightening

Aligning Rear Drop-outs

Tools and equipment:
vice with soft metal
protectors, mounted on a
work bench

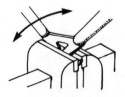

4.6 Drop-out straightening

3 Repeat step 2 for the LH drop-out.

4. Compare the distance of the straightedge from the seat tube on both sides, referring to the dimension lines shown in Fig. 4.7.

5. Measure the distance between the drop-outs and compare it with the sum of the seat tube diameter and the two distances just measured.

6. If the difference is more than 3 mm (⅛ in), at least one of the drop-outs should be straightened — preferably by the bike mechanic, but you may want to try your hand at it yourself. Usually, you can tell by means of a visual inspection which is the one that's bent.

After the preceding check, you may want to straighten a bent drop-out. However, don't do it if cracks are visible at any point or if the derailleur mounting lug (with its threaded hole) is bent relative to the rest of the drop-out. Leave such problems to the bike mechanic, who has a special tool for this job. The same goes for composite and aluminum frames — the aluminum drop-outs used on those tend to crack, if not when they get bent in the first place, then when you try to straighten them.

Procedure:
1. Establish whether it is just the derailleur eye or the dropout itself that is bent. In the latter case, check which drop-out has to be bent in which direction, by checking carefully from behind and from the top when the wheel has been removed from the bike.

2. Clamp the drop-out to be straightened in the vice right up to the location of the bend. Alternatively, you can use two 8-inch adjustable wrenches, one on either side of the bend.

3. Force the frame in the appropriate direction, using the bike (or the adjustable wrenches) for leverage.

4. Check again and make any corrections that may be necessary.

Touching up Paint Damage

Tools and equipment:
touch-up paint, brush, cloth, sandpaper, paint thinner

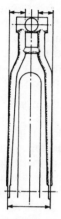

4.7 Rear triangle alignment check

In off-road use, you can't help but scratch up your bike sometimes. At least once a season, it will be worthwhile to touch up any nicks and scratches.

Procedure:
1.   Clean the bike thoroughly, to uncover any locations that may have to be touched up.

2.   Sand down the area of the damage, folding the sandpaper into such a thin pad, that you remove as little good paint as possible.

3.   Clean the area with a dry rag, then with paint thinner, treating only the small area immediately affected, and again with a clean, dry rag.

4.   Dip the paint brush in the paint very sparingly, and treat only the area where the paint has been removed, minimizing any overlapping over paint that is still intact.

5.   Clean the brush in paint thinner immediately after use and allow to dry suspended with the bristles down but not touching anything.

6.   Allow to dry at least overnight before touching the frame again.

Note 1:   If you can only get paint in a spraycan, spray a little in a bottle cap and dip the brush in it.

Note 2:   Do not touch any bonded or composite frame with paint thinner or other solvents, since that may weaken the joints.

Chapter 5
The Steering System

The steering system is crucial for the control over the bike. This is even more important on an off-road bike than it is on any other kind of bicycle. It is also subjected to more abuse under off-road conditions, so its maintenance is quite important.

The parts of the steering system are depicted in Fig. 5.1: front fork, headset bearings, stem and handlebars (the latter two parts sometimes combined into a single welded unit on some models). We'll cover each of the components, starting at the most frequently necessary jobs.

Handlebars and Stem

The handlebars are generally clamped in the stem by means of a binder, or clamping, bolt and the stem is held in the fork's steerer tube, as shown in Fig. 5.2, by means of a wedge-shaped (or more rarely a cone-shaped) device. This is pulled into the bottom of the stem with the expander bolt, accessible from the top of the stem and usually equipped with a 6 mm hexagon recess for an Allen key. Allen bolts are also used to clamp the handlebars in the stem.

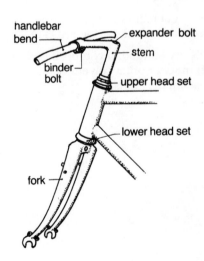

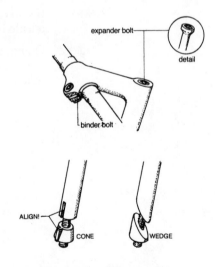

5.1 Parts of the steering system

5.2 Handlebar and stem clamping details

The jobs most typically required are adjusting the height, straightening the bars, and replacement of either part. Most mountain bike handlebars are 7/8 in. (22.2 mm) diameter, with a 1 in. (25.4 mm) or sometimes 1 1/8 in. (26.6 mm) bulge where it is clamped into the stem. Make sure stem and handlebars match when replacing either one.

Adjusting or Tightening Handlebars

This is required when the bike is set up for a different rider, when the position proves uncomfortable, or when the handlebars are not firmly in place.

Tools and equipment:
Allen key, sometimes a mallet or a hammer

Procedure:
1. If the front brake cable is anchored at the stem, first loosen the brake (see Chapter 10) to relax the cable.

2. If appropriate (i.e. to adjust), loosen the attachment of the stem by unscrewing the expander bolt 2–3 turns.

3. Straddle the front wheel, keeping it straight relative to the bike's frame, and put the handlebars in the required position as regards height and orientation, holding it steady there with one hand.

4. If the thing won't turn or move, unscrew the expander bolt two more turns, lift the wheel off the ground, supporting the bike from the handlebars, then tap on the expander bolt with the mallet, after which it will usually come loose. If it doesn't, enter some spray lubricant between the stem and the collar or locknut at the top of the headset and try again.

5. Still holding firmly, tighten the expander bolt.

6. Verify whether the handlebars are now in the right position and make any corrections that may be necessary.

7. If the brake's adjustment was affected (see step 1 above), tension the cable and adjust the brake as outlined in Chapter 10.

Tightening Handlebars in Stem

The connection between the handlebars and the stem should also be firm, so the handlebars don't twist out of their proper orientation. Do this by simply tightening the bolts that clamp the stem collar around the bars, using a matching Allen key.

Replacing Handlebars with Stem

This has to be done when the bars are bent or otherwise damaged, when you want to install a different design, or in the context of a general overhauling operation of the bike.

Tools and equipment:
Allen key, rag, lubricant

Removal procedure:
1. Loosen all cables leading to items installed on the handlebars (gear and brake levers), as explained in the relevant chapters 9 and 10.

2. Using the Allen key, loosen the expander bolt by 3–4 turns, or until the stem is obviously loose.

3. If the stem won't come loose, unscrew the expander bolt two more turns, lift the wheel off the ground, holding the bike by the handlebars, then tap on the expander bolt with the mallet, after which it will usually come loose. If it doesn't, enter some spray lubricant between the stem and the collar or locknut at the top of the headset and try again.

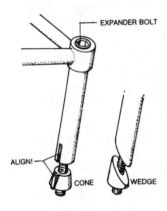

4. Remove the handlebars complete with the stem.

Installation procedure:
1. Clean the stem and the inside of the fork's steerer tube with a clean rag, and then put some vaseline on the wedge (or the cone) and the part of the stem that will go inside the steerer tube, in order to prevent rust and to ease subsequent adjustment or replacement.

5.3 Stem details

2. Tighten the expander bolt so far that the wedge is snug up to the stem's slanted end in the right orientation, still allowing free movement of the stem in the steerer tube.

3. If a cone-shape device is used instead of a wedge, align the ribs on the cone with the slots in the end of the stem.

4. Install the stem and position it in the correct orientation.

5. Straddle the front wheel, keeping it straight relative to the bike's frame, and put the handlebars in the required position as regards height and orientation, holding it steady there with one hand.

6. Still holding the handlebars firmly in place, tighten the expander bolt.

7. Verify whether the handlebars are now in the right position and make any corrections that may be necessary.

8. If the brake's adjustment was affected (see step 1 above), tension the cable and adjust the brake as described in Chapter 10.

Replacing Handlebars or Stem

This must be done when the handlebars are seriously damaged or when you want to install another model. First check whether the new handlebars have the same diameter as the old ones — if not, you should also replace the stem, following the preceding instruction instead.

Tools and equipment:
Allen key, large screwdriver, tools to replace items installed on the handlebars

Removal procedure:
1. Remove any components installed on the handlebars: handgrips, brake levers, gear shifters — after first releasing tension in the cables, as explained in Chapter 9 for the gear shifters, Chapter 10 for the brake levers.

2. Loosen and remove the binder bolts clamping the stem around the handlebars.

3. Using the big screwdriver, spread open the collar and pull the thicker section of the handlebars out of the collar; then release the screwdriver and if necessary twist the handlebars in such a way as to find the most favorable orientation if it is hard to pull out.

Installation procedure:
1. Push the handlebars through the collar, twisting if necessary, until the thicker section is reached, then open up the collar with the big screwdriver.

2. Bring the handlebars to the correct location.

3. Install the bolts and tighten them partway.

4. Adjust the bars in the exact location desired and hold them there firmly, while tightening the bolts.

5. Install all the components required on the handlebars, following the appropriate instructions in the relevant chapters.

6. Check the position and orientation again, making any adjustments that may be necessary.

Shortening Handlebars

Some mountain bikes are still supplied with overly wide handlebars. If you are not unusually big, you may want to shorten them to about 55 cm (22 in.) but certainly no more than 60 cm (24 in.) total width. This can be done once they are installed, using a metal saw. Wind some handlebar tape around the bars at the desired cut location to use as a guide to make sure you cut them straight.

Tools and equipment:
hacksaw, file

First remove handgrips and measure off the same distance both sides, marking the location to be cut with a marking pen. Stand in such a position that you can cut perfectly square, and preferably do it while someone else holds bike and handlebars firmly in position. File the rough cutting edge smooth. Finally reinstall all components.

Replacing Handgrips

You may want to replace the handgrips for a more comfortable model or you will have to remove them when replacing the bars without the stem.

Tools and equipment:
small screwdriver, rag, dishwashing liquid, hot water, hairspray

Lift the ends of the grips off the handlebars a little with the small screwdriver and enter some dishwashing liquid if they won't come off easily (they shouldn't, since it might be dangerous when riding, if you suddenly hold a wayward handgrip instead of retaining control over the handlebars). Before reinstalling the handgrips, remove all traces of dishwashing liquid, so they won't slide off. To install, dip the handgrips in hot water before forcing them over the handlebars. To prevent the handgrips from slipping off, spray hairspray inside before installation.

Bar Ends

Many riders feel the regular mountain bike handlebars too restrictive and decide to install bar-ends (also called bull horns) at the ends. The safest models have a clamp that works just like the device that holds the stem in the steerer tube. First cut back the ends of the handgrips and then install the bar ends by tightening the Allen bolt that pulls the wedge inside the handlebar ends — firmly enough so they don't slip under load.

The Headset

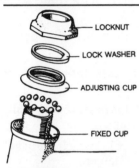

5.4 Headset adjusting details

Shown in Fig. 5.4 and 5.5, this is the double set of ball bearings with which the steering system is pivoted in the frame. By way of regular maintenance, it should occasionally be lubricated and perhaps overhauled, or — when it can't be adjusted to satisfaction — it may have to be replaced.

Mountain bike headsets come in a variety of sizes — regular 1 in. and both 1⅛ and 1¼ in. oversize types — and at least one manufacturer (Klein) has its own proprietary model. Make sure you use tools and replacement parts of the size for the model in question.

Adjusting Headset

Once a season — and whenever the steering is rough or loose — adjust the bearings as follows:

Tools and equipment:
headset wrench or large crescent wrench

Procedure:
1. Loosen the collar or locknut on the upper headset by about one turn (after loosening a grub screws on models with such a device).

2. Lift the washer under this nut enough to release the underlying part, which is the adjustable bearing cup.

3. Tighten or loosen the adjustable bearing cup by turning it in the appropriate direction if the bearing is too loose or too tight, respectively.

4. Put the washer in place and tighten the collar or locknut.

5. Check to make sure the adjustment is correct; readjust if necessary, following the same procedure.

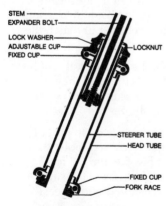

5.5 Parts of the headset

Note: If adjusting does not solve your problem, the headset must be overhauled according to the following description.

Overhauling Headset

The same disassembly and installation procedures are followed when either the headset or the fork is to be replaced.

Tools and equipment:
headset tools or large crescent wrench, tools to remove handlebars and brake, bearing grease, rags

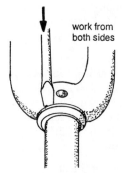

work from
both sides

5.6 Fork race removal

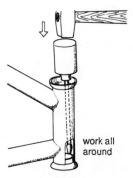

work all
around

5.7 Fixed cup removal

Disassembly procedure:
1.   Remove the handlebars with the stem as described above and loosen the front brake cable; then remove the front wheel, after unhooking or relaxing tension on the front brake cable.

2.   Loosen and remove the collar or locknut on top of the headset

3.   Remove the lockwasher by lifting it straight off.

4.   Unscrew the adjustable bearing cup, while holding the fork to the frame.

5.   Remove the bearing balls, which are usually held in a bearing ball retainer.

6.   Pull the fork out from the frame, also catching the lower bearing balls, again usually held in a retainer.

Inspection and overhauling procedure:
1.   Inspect all parts for wear, corrosion and damage, evidenced as pitting or grooves.

2.   Replace the entire headset if significant damage is apparent; always take new bearing balls, either loose or in a retainer to match the particular size of headset installed.

3.   If the headset has to be replaced, it will be preferable to get the fixed cups and the fork race removed (and new ones installed) with special tools at the bike shop.

4.   Should you have the desire to do part of this job yourself using improvised tools, proceed as outlined in Fig. 5.6 and 5.7 to remove the fork race and the fixed bearing cup. Get the new ones installed with special tools at the bike shop.

Installation procedure:

1. If the fixed cups and the fork race are intact — or once they have been replaced — fill the bearing cups with bearing grease.

2. Hold the frame upside down and embed one of the bearing retainers in the grease-filled lower fixed bearing race (which is now facing up). The retainer must be installed in such a way that the bearing balls — not the metal ring — contact the inside of the cup.

3. Hold the fork upside-down and put it through the head tube.

4. Turn the frame the right way round again.

5. Embed the other bearing retainer in the grease-filled upper fixed bearing cup.

6. Screw the adjustable bearing cup on the threaded end of the fork's steerer tube by hand.

7. Place the lock washer on top of the adjustable cup, and do the same with any part that may be installed to serve as a brake cable anchor.

8. Screw the collar or locknut onto the threaded end of the steerer tube, without tightening it completely.

9. Install the front wheel.

10. Adjust the bearing as outlined above.

11. Check and, if necessary, correct any adjustments involved: handlebars and front brake.

The Front Fork

Fig. 5.8 shows the mountain bike's front fork. Though other versions are around, the majority of production mountain bikes use the unicrown design depicted. But be aware that there are differences, primarily on account of the headset bearing used: regular or one of several oversize steerer tube diameters.

If the steering gets sticky when turning the bars, even though it seems fine when going straight, it will be due to a bent head tube, usually as a result of a collision. When replacing a fork that is bent, make sure the bosses installed for the brakes are in the right location for the kind of brakes used, and check the length of the steerer tube, which must also be the same as the old one—assuming it is correct. You can follow Fig. 5.10 to establish the correct length by adding the stacking height of the headset to the length of the head tube and deducting 2 mm (3/32 in.).

Front Fork Inspection

This will be necessary whenever you have had a serious crash or when the bike does not seem to steer the way it should. Generally, a visual check is adequate, referring to Fig. 5.9 for the typical kinds of damage possible.

Replacing Front Fork

Though it may sometimes be possible to straighten a bent fork, I suggest that it will be smarter to replace the entire fork, giving you a sorely needed margin of safety that may prevent a bad crash later on. Sometimes the fork's steerer tube has to be cut shorter to fit the frame. It is preferable to get that done at the bike shop, since the screw thread often has to be recut too. If you do decide to do it yourself, first screw the locknut on as a guide so you'll cut straight. File any burrs off the end before installing the fork.

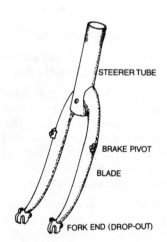

5.8 Fork details

5.9 Fork damage

Tools and equipment:
large crescent wrench or headset tool, tools to remove handlebars and front brake.

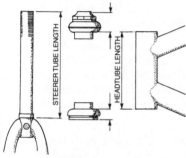

5.10 Steerer tube length and headset stacking height

Special Headsets

Suspension

Procedure:

1. Untension the cable for the front brake and remove the entire front brake as explained in Chapter 10; then remove the front wheel following the appropriate procedure in Chapter 7.

2. Remove the handlebars with the stem, following the description in this chapter.

3. Disassemble the upper headset as outlined in the relevant description above.

4. Remove the fork, following the same description.

5. If necessary, use the fork as a reference to buy the new one, taking it to the bike shop with you.

6. Install the fork and the headset as described for the installation of the headset.

7. Install the handlebars as described above.

8. Install the front brake and hook up the cable.

9. Check and, if necessary, adjust all parts affected: headset, handlebars, front brake.

Recently, a special headset for use with matching fork and stem has become popular. On this AHeadSet, the stem is clamped directly to the fork's steerer tube, but it is maintained just like other models.

The most significant development of the mountain bike in recent years has been the introduction of suspension systems. Usually, they take the form of a special fork with shock absorber built in, sometimes a sprung stem may be used instead.

As far as maintenance is concerned, the latter require no more than checking the connections. The former, however require very careful attention, which is best left to the bike shop. They vary considerably between makes and models, so any maintenance instructions, which can be obtained from the manufacturer, must be for the exact model in question.

Chapter 6
Saddle and Seatpost

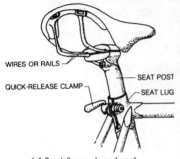

WIRES OR RAILS

QUICK-RELEASE CLAMP

SEAT POST

SEAT LUG

6.1 Saddle and seatpost

Although these are not amongst the most trouble-prone components on the mountain bike, they do justify some attention. The jobs described here will be adjustment of the position of the saddle (also called seat), replacement of saddle and seatpost and any maintenance needed on a leather saddle. The Hite-Rite adjusting aid, installed on many top-quality mountain bikes, is described in Chapter 11, which deals with accessories.

Fig. 6.1 shows the saddle and the seatpost installed on the bike, while in Fig. 6.2 the various types of seatpost are illustrated. On the mountain bike, the binder bolt generally takes the form of a quick-release mechanism, which is shown in Fig. 6.3.

The saddle position should be adjusted whenever the bike is set up for another rider or when the position is uncomfortably high or low. My *Mountain Bike Book* explains in detail how the correct height is determined.

Adjusting Saddle Height

In this and the following descriptions, I shall merely explain how the actual adjustment operations are carried out, assuming you know how high you want it to be.

Tools and Equipment:
usually none required
(sometimes lubricant)

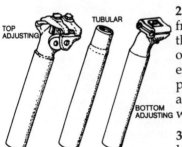

TOP ADJUSTING

TUBULAR

BOTTOM ADJUSTING

6.2 Seatpost types

1. Flip the lever of the quick-release binder bolt in the open position in order to loosen the seatpost.

2. The seatpost with the saddle should now be free to move up and down. If it is not, hold the lever and unscrew the thumbnut on the other side by about one turn. If it still isn't, enter some liquid lubricant between the seatpost and the seat lug, wait a minute or two and try again, if necessary twisting the saddle with the seatpost relative to the frame.

3. Place the saddle in the desired location (if lubrication was needed, first remove it all the way, then clean the seatpost and the interior of the seat tube and apply some grease or vaseline to the outside of the seatpost)

4. Holding the saddle at the correct height, and aligned perfectly straight forward, flip the quick-release lever in the closed position.

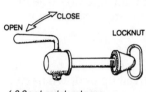

6.3 Seat quick-release

5. Check whether the saddle is now installed firmly. If not, loosen the quick-release lever, tighten the thumbnut perhaps one turn, and try again.

6. Try out and readjust if necessary until the location is satisfactory.

Note: If your bike has a Hite-Rite spring adjuster, apply just enough downward force on the saddle to achieve the desired location when adjusting. If the range of the Hite-Rite is incorrect for the required saddle position, undo the clamp around the seatpost and attach it higher or lower as required. Refer to Chapter 11 for additional details.

Adjusting Saddle Angle and Position

Generally, both these adjustments are carried out with the same bolts that hold the saddle to the seatpost, which can be reached from under the saddle (except on some special seatposts, such as the Campagnolo Euclid model, which has an adjustment by means of a large knurled button and an additional quick-release — a mild case of overkill).

Tools and equipment:
Allen key or other wrench to fit seatpost adjusting bolts

Procedure:
1. If the saddle must be moved forward or backward, loosen both bolts by about one or two turns each.

2. Holding the clamp on top of the seatpost with one hand and the saddle with the other; now move the latter in the correct position.

3. If the saddle merely has to be tipped, the front raised or lowered relative to the rear portion, loosen the nuts, and then move the saddle in the correct orientation.

6.4 Twisting saddle to loosen

4. Holding the saddle in the correct location and orientation, tighten the bolts, making sure the saddle does not move while doing so.

5.   Check and readjust if necessary.

Replacing Saddle with Seatpost

It is usually easier to remove the combination of saddle and seatpost than to remove the saddle alone. This is also the first step in removing the seatpost.

Tools and Equipment:
rag, grease or vaseline (sometimes wrench for Hite-Rite bolt)

Removal procedure:
1. Loosen the quick-release binder bolt until the seatpost can be moved up or down freely, as described under *Adjust Saddle Height.*

2. Pull the saddle with the seatpost out of the frame's seat tube.

Installation procedure:
1. Clean the outside of the seatpost and the inside of the seat tube, than smear grease or vaseline on the seatpost to prevent corrosion and to ease subsequent adjustments.

2. Install the seatpost with the saddle installed and adjust it at the correct height.

3. In case you are installing it with a Hite-Rite, clamp it around the seatpost when it is perfectly aligned and about 1.5 cm (⅝ in.) higher than you will ever want the saddle to be.

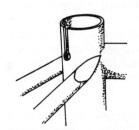
6.5 Slot in back of seat lug

4. Tighten the quick-release binder bolt as described under Adjusting Saddle Height.

Note: If adjustment problems persist, especially if the seatpost won't come loose, it may be necessary to drill out the hole at the bottom of the slot in the rear of the seat lug to about 3 mm (⅛ in.) as shown in Fig 6.5 — or drill such a hole there if there is not one, since it prevents the formation of cracks and eases clamping or unclamping the lug around the seatpost.

Replacing Seatpost or Saddle

Not exactly a job that is often necessary, except if a new saddle or seatpost has to be installed — or to get water out of the frame. Just the same, here's how to go about it.

Tools and equipment:
Allen key or other wrench to fit bolts that hold saddle to seatpost, sometimes wrench for Hite-Rite nut

Removal procedure:
1. For the time being, leave the saddle installed on the seatpost and remove the seatpost complete with the saddle as described under Replace Saddle with Seat-

post, loosening the Hite-Rite clamp around the seatpost if installed.

2. Separate the saddle from the seatpost by unscrewing the bolts that hold the saddle's wires to the seatpost clamp.

Installation procedure:
1. Install the saddle on the seatpost.

2. Install the seatpost with the saddle as described under Replace Saddle with Seatpost, entering the seatpost through the Hite-Rite if appropriate.

3. In case you are installing it with a Hite-Rite, clamp it around the seatpost when it is about as high as you will ever want the saddle to be.

4. Adjust the height, the forward position and the angle of the saddle as described in the relevant sections above.

5. Check and readjust if necessary.

Maintenance of Leather Saddle

If you use a real leather saddle (as opposed to the usual nylon one with a thin leather cover), make sure it does not get wet. Wrap a plastic bag around the saddle when transporting the bike or leaving it outside when there is the slightest chance of rain. If it does get wet, don't sit on it until it is thoroughly dried out, since otherwise it will deform permanently. To keep it water resistant and slightly flexible, treat it with leather treatment such as Brooks Proofide at least twice a year.

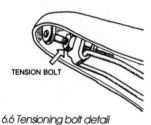

TENSION BOLT

6.6 Tensioning bolt detail

Adjust the tension of a leather saddle no more than once a year and only when it is noticeable sagged, tightening the bolt shown in Fig. 6.6 perhaps one turn at the most. Don't overdo this adjustment, since it often causes the saddle to be pulled into an uncomfortable shape.

Installing Sprung Leather Saddle

The most comfortable leather saddles, such as the Brooks ATB Conquest, have double wires and coil springs. To install this kind of saddle on a regular seatpost, you will have to install a filler piece between the wires in the saddle. Breeze and Angel, manufacturers of the Hite-Rite, also offer such a filler piece, illustrated in

Fig 6.7. Place it (or a home-made substitute) between the saddle's two pairs of wires and between the seatpost's main part and its clamp, then tighten the bolts and adjust the saddle as described above.

6.7 Double-wire saddle mounting adaptor

Chapter 7
The Wheels

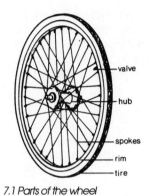

7.1 *Parts of the wheel*

Fig. 7.1 shows the bicycle wheel and the parts that make it up. These are hub, tire, tube (not visible here, since it is contained in the tire), and spokes. The spokes are hooked onto the flanges of the hub and connected with the rim by means of screwed-on nipples. The ends of the spokes and the nipples are covered with an also invisible strip of rim tape to protect the tube.

A fairly high percentage of the kind of mishaps that puts your mountain bike out of commission temporarily is attributable to wheel problems, especially if you actually ride off-road frequently. In this chapter we shall cover all the major maintenance and repair operations required.

In the following sections, you will be shown how to replace the wheel most effectively, as is often necessary to transport the bike or to carry out other maintenance jobs.

Replacing Wheel With Quick-Release

Tools and equipment: sometimes rag for rear wheel

Quick-release hubs are by now used almost exclusively on mountain bikes. Refer to Fig. 7.2 for the operation of the quick-release.

Removal procedure:

1. If you are working on the rear wheel, first put the chain on the smallest sprocket and the smallest chainring by means of the derailleur, while turning the cranks with the wheel raised off the ground.

2. To allow the tire to pass between the brake pads (unless you have a flat), release the brake by squeezing the brake arms against the rim and unhooking one of the cable nipples (on cantilever brake or U-brake) or by twisting the cam plate out (on the roller-cam brake). In the case of an under-the-chainstay U-brake, just push the wheel forward in the drop-outs until it hits the inside of the brake, which will spread the brake arms apart.

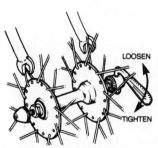

7.2 *Quick-release operation*

3. Twist the lever on the quick-release in the *open* position.

4. On the rear wheel, pull back the derailleur and the chain as illustrated in Fig. 7.3.

5. Pull out the wheel, guiding it past the brake pads.

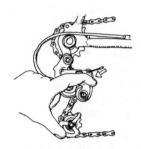

7.3 Holding back derailleur

Installation procedure:
1. If you are working on the rear wheel, first put the shifters in the position to engage the gear with the chain on the smallest sprocket and the smallest chainring (turn the cranks forward if you have to engage another chainring in the front).

2. To allow the tire to pass between the brake pads, make sure the the brake is released — if not, squeeze the brake arms together and un-hook one of the cable nipples (on cantilever brake or U-brake) or twist the cam plate out (on the roller-cam brake).

3. Twist the lever on the hub's quick-release in the *open* position.

4. On the rear wheel, pull back the derailleur and the chain as illustrated in Fig. 7.3.

5. Slide the wheel back into position, guiding it past the brake pads.

6. Straighten the wheel exactly between fork blades or chain stays and seat stays.

7. Holding the wheel in the correct position, flip the quick-release lever in the *closed* position and make sure the wheel is locked firmly in place (see note below).

8. Check whether you have installed the wheel perfectly centered and correct if necessary.

9. Tension the brake or reinstall the cable nipple, then readjust the brake to make sure the brake pads touch the sides of the rim fully when the brake lever is applied

Note: If the quick-release does not tighten the wheel properly, or conversely, if it does not fit clear of the drop-outs, put the lever in the *open* position and unscrew or tighten the

Replacing Wheel with Axle Nuts

Tools and equipment:
wrench to fit axle nuts; for rear wheel: rag

7.4 Axle nut detail

thumbnut by perhaps one turn, then try again.

Still used on some mountain bikes, the attachment by means of axle nuts is in no way inferior. Here's how to go about removing and installing such a wheel.

Removal procedure

1. If you are working on the rear wheel, first put the chain on the smallest sprocket and the smallest chainring by means of the derailleur, while turning the cranks with the rear wheel raised off the ground.

2. To allow the tire to pass between the brake pads (unless you have a flat), release the brake by squeezing the brake arms against the rim and unhook one of the cable nipples (on cantilever brake or U-brake) or twist the cam plate out (on the roller-cam brake). On a bike with under-the-chainstay U-brake, push the wheel forward against the inside of the brake to spread the brake arms apart.

3. Loosen both axle nuts by two or three turns.

4. On the rear wheel, pull back the derailleur and the chain as illustrated in Fig. 7.3.

5. Pull out the wheel, guiding it past the brake pads.

Installation procedure:

1. If you are working on the rear wheel, first put the shifters in the position to engage the gear with the chain on the smallest sprocket and the smallest chainring (turn the cranks forward if you have to engage another chainring in the front).

2. To allow the tire to pass between the brake pads, make sure the the brake is released — if not, squeeze the brake arms together and unhook one of the cable nipples (on cantilever brake or U-brake) or twist the cam plate out (on the roller-cam brake).

3. Install the washers (if the axle nuts do not have integral washers) between the dropouts and the nuts.

4. On the rear wheel, pull back the derailleur and the chain as illustrated in Fig. 7.3.

5. Slide the wheel back into position, guiding it past the brake pads, and center the rim exactly between fork blades or between chain stays and seat stays.

6. Holding the wheel in place at the brake, first tighten the axle nuts one after the other by hand, then tighten them fully with the wrench.

7. Verify you have installed the wheel in the right position and correct if necessary.

8. Tension the brake or reinstall the cable nipple, then readjust the brake to make sure the brake pads touch the sides of the rim fully when the brake lever is applied

The Hub

Fig. 7.5 is a cross section through a typical wheel hub. The mountain bike's hubs should be checked occasionally to make sure they still turn freely and are not too loose. Maintenance will consist of adjustment, lubrication and overhauling when necessary. These operations will have to be left to the bike shop's mechanic if the hub in question has so-called sealed bearings (which are more correctly called non-adjustable cartridge bearings), instead of the more common adjustable cup-and-cone bearings illustrated.

It makes a lot of sense to maximize the life of a hub by means of frequent checks, adjustment, lubrication and overhauling: To replace a hub, the entire wheel has to be rebuilt, which runs

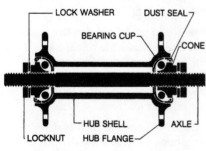

7.5 Cross section through hub

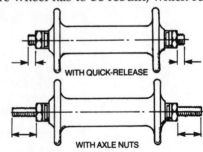

7.6 Axle protrusion details

the bill up considerably. Besides, often hubs are often only available as pairs, effectively doubling the cost.

Hub Bearing Check

This procedure applies to any kind of hub. regardless whether it is the conventional adjustable bearing type or a cartridge bearing model.

Tools and Equipment:
usually none required

Procedure:
1.   To check whether the hub runs freely, lift the wheel off the ground and let it spin slowly. It should rotate several times and then oscillate gradually into the motionless state with the (slightly heavier) valve at the bottom. If it does not turn freely, the bearings should be adjusted to loosen them (and probably they should be lubricated).

2.   To check whether there is no play in the bearings, grab the rim close to the brake, countering at the fork or the stays, and try to push it sideways in both directions. If it moves loosely, the bearing should be tightened somewhat.

Adjusting Hub Bearings

Carry out this work when the preceding test indicates a need for readjustment. It applies to cup-and-cone bearings only. In the case of a rear hub, first remove the freewheel (see Chapter 8), unless it is a cassette type hub.

Tools and equipment:
cone wrenches, wrench to fit locknuts, tools to remove wheel

Procedure:
1.   Remove the wheel or — if it is the type with axle nuts — at least loosen the axle nut on one side if you want to leave the wheel installed on the bike.

2.   Loosen the locknut on one side by one turn, countering at the cone on the same side of the wheel with the cone wrench

3.   Tighten or loosen the cone by about ¼ turn at a time until the bearing is just a little loose. To loosen, counter at the cone on the other side with an open-ended wrench. To tighten, counter at the *locknut* on the other side.

4.   Hold the cone with the cone wrench and tighten the locknut hard up against it, which will slightly decrease the play, justifying the

advice given in point 3 to keep it just a little loose.

5.   Check and readjust if necessary.

6.   Reinstall the wheel in the bike — or just tighten the axle nut if you only loosened it on one side.

Lubricating Hub Bearing

Once a season, or whenever adjusting does not solve the hub's problems, lubricate the hub in a big way as described below under *Overhaul Hub*. In between, many high-quality hubs can be quickly lubricated through an oil hole provided in the hub shell, which is covered by a spring clip. Use SAE 60 or thicker oil, filled in a pressure oil can with a very narrow spout. Other bearings can be stuffed with grease after the plastic seals are lifted with a narrow screwdriver.

Overhauling Hub

Do this work when the bearings of the hub are no longer running smoothly and cannot be returned to proper working order by means of adjustment and lubrication.

Tools and equipment:
cone wrenches, wrenches to fit locknuts, rags, grease

Disassembly procedure:
1.   Remove the wheel from the bike, following the appropriate description in this chapter.

2.   Remove the quick-release skewer or the axle nuts and washers.

3.   Remove the locknut on one side, countering at the cone on the *same* side.

4.   Lift off the lock washer.

5.   Remove the cone, countering at the cone on the other side, and catching the bearing balls as you remove it.

6   Pull the axle (with the other cone, washer and locknut still installed at the other end) out of the hub shell, again catching the bearing balls and removing the plastic seal (if installed) from the hub shell.

Overhauling procedure:
1.   Clean and inspect all bearing parts.

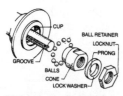

7.7 Bearing adjustment

2. Replace the bearing balls (make sure you get balls of the same size) and any other parts that may be damaged, as evidenced by pitted, grooved or corroded surfaces.

Reassembly procedure:
1. First fill the clean bearing cups in the hub with bearing grease, then reinstall the plastic dust seals, if applicable.

2. Push the bearing balls into the grease, filling the circumference but leaving just enough space for them to move freely (i.e. usually one ball less than might fit in a pinch).

3. Insert the axle with one cone, washer and locknut still installed; on a rear wheel, make sure it goes the same way round as it was originally.

4. Screw the other cone on the free axle end until the bearing seems just a little loose.

5. Install the lock washer with its prong, or key, in the groove in the axle.

6. Screw the locknut on and tighten it against the cone.

7. Check and, if necessary, adjust the bearing as described above until it runs satisfactorily.

8. Reinstall the wheel in the bike.

Note: If parts that are screwed onto the axle are replaced, make sure the axle protrudes equally far on both sides — reposition both cones and locknuts to achieve this if necessary.

Rim and Spokes

These two parts have to be treated together, since the spoke tension determines largely whether the rim is straight and true or not. They are shown in Fig. 7.8 and 7.9, respectively. The spokes connect the rim to the hub in one of the patterns shown in Fig. 7.10, referred to as 3-cross and 4-cross spoking, respectively. Other patterns may be equally suitable for the front wheel, which does not transmit any moments, as the rear wheel does when it is driven.

The way to minimize wheel problems — most typically broken spokes or a bent rim — is to

BOX SECTION   CENTER WELL
              SECTION

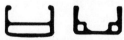

7.8 Rim cross sections

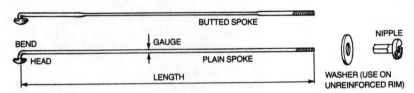

7.9 Spoke details

Wheel Truing Check

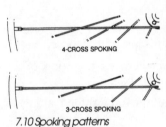

7.10 Spoking patterns

Emergency Repair of Buckled Wheel

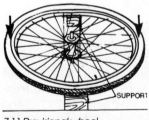

7.11 Provisional wheel straightening

Wheel Truing

keep the spokes tensioned evenly and adequately. Check the feel and the sound of plucking a well tensioned new wheel at a bike shop and compare yours. If necessary, increase the tension of all or specific spokes, following the procedure outlined in the following section on wheel truing.

When a wheel is damaged, the rim is often permanently deformed sideways, resulting in wheel wobble. When riding, you will notice this as lateral oscillations. It may be verified by turning the wheel slowly while it is lifted off the ground, observing the distance between the rim and a fixed point on the frame's rear triangle or on the fork, for a rear wheel and a front wheel, respectively. On a properly trued wheel, this distance is the same on both sides of the wheel and does not vary as the wheel is turned.

Sometimes the damage is so serious that you don't need to check: it will be obvious that the wheel is buckled into the shape of a pretzel — and there is little you can do to solve the problem permanently or even temporarily with adequate certainty to be safe. Just the same, such a seriously bent wheel can often be straightened enough to ride home — carefully.

Support the wheel at the low point and push down forcefully on the high points, as illustrated in Fig. 7.11. Check frequently and continue until the whole thing at least looks like a wheel more than like the product of a Jewish bakery. Then follow the procedure for *Wheel Truing* to fine-tune the wheel far enough to be able to ride it home. Have it corrected or replaced as soon as possible.

This is the work done to get a bent wheel back into shape. It is most easily done at home, but can be carried out after a fashion by the road-

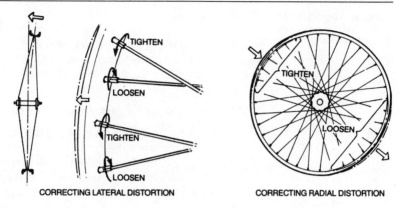

CORRECTING LATERAL DISTORTION   CORRECTING RADIAL DISTORTION

7.12 Wheel truing procedure

side or off-road — at least well enough to get you home. Refer to Fig. 7.12.

Tools and equipment:
spoke wrench (or small adjustable wrench).

Procedure:
1. Slowly spin the wheel while watching a fixed reference point on both sides, as described under *Wheel Truing Check*. Mark the locations that have to be moved further to the left and the right, respectively.

2. Using the spoke wrench, loosen the nipples of the spokes on the high side in the area of a high spot, tighten those on the opposite side, in that area. Turn the ones in the middle of the high spot ½ turn, those further from the center only ¼ turn at a time (this is easy, since the nipples have a square flattened area for the tool).

3. Continue this process for each off-set area, checking and correcting frequently, until the wheel is quite well trued.

Note: The first time you do this, it will take forever and a day and still may not lead to a really satisfactory result. Persist, and the next time will be easier. Just the same, have a bike mechanic go over it when you get home to make sure the wheel will last.

Replacing Spokes

Sometimes a spoke breaks — usually at the head, which is hooked in at the hub flange. Make sure you have replacement spokes of the same thickness and the same length.

Tools and equipment:
spoke wrench, sometimes tools to remove freewheel.

Procedure:

1. Unscrew the remaining end from the nipple. If that is not possible, let air out of the tire, lift tire, tube and rim tape local to the spoke nipple, and remove it to install the new nipple.

2. Hook the spoke through the hole in the hub.

3. Count four spokes over along the circumference of the rim for a spoke that is routed the same way as your spoke will have to be. Refer to this one to find out just how to run it and how it should cross which other spokes.

4. Route your spoke the same way as suggested by the example.

5. Screw the nipple onto the threaded end of the spoke, slowly increasing tension until it is about as tight as all other spokes on the same side of the same wheel.

6. Follow the procedure given under *Wheel Truing* until the wheel is perfectly true.

Note: If several spokes are broken, figure out which rim hole goes with which hub hole by observing that every fourth spoke along the rim, and every second one on the same hub flange, runs similarly.

Emergency Spoke Installation

You can make an emergency spoke from an oversized spoke with the head cut off and bent as shown in Fig. 7.13. It is useful when a spoke on the RH side of the rear wheel breaks, since it can be hooked in without removing the freewheel.

Note: When you get home, replace this temporary repair by a permanent spoke of the right length, a job you can either do yourself or leave to the bike shop.

Tire and Tube

Fig. 7.14 illustrates a typical tire as installed on a mountain bike. The tire size is marked on the

7.13 Emergency spoke

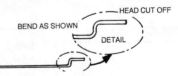

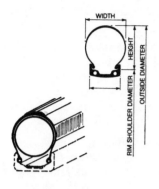

7.14 Tire details

sidewall and must match the rim. On virtually all mountain bikes, rims with a diameter of 559 mm are used, requiring tires of a corresponding size. Though their international standard size (ISO or ETRTO designation) references this rim diameter and the width of the cross section, the US and its Far Eastern suppliers have been reluctant to use this system. Instead, mountain bike tires are usually designated as 26 inches, times whatever nominal width they have.

The width of the tire is important in matching machine and terrain: though relatively narrow tires are acceptable for riding on well-surfaced roads, the wider versions with a nominal width of 2.125 or even 2.2 in. are needed for really rough terrain, as well as for loose sand, snow or other soft surfaces. Not every tire width can necessarily be installed on every mountain bike frame or every mountain bike rim: when installed, there should be at least 5 mm (³⁄₁₆ in.) clearance between inflated tire and frame stays or fork blades on both sides. The inner tube should ideally match the tire, though you will find that most tubes fit most tires, whatever their nominal width.

The tires remain the week spot, even on the mountain bike with its rugged tires.

Puncture Repair

Fixing a punctured or 'flat' tire is required more frequently than any other repair, and every cyclist should be able to handle this simple job. Whether you actually fix the old tube or install a new one is up to you, but you can't carry unlimited spares, so you will be confronted with the need to actually fix the leak yourself sooner or later. Although the description involves many steps, the work is not difficult and can, with some practice, be handled in about ten minutes, even out on the trail.

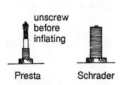

7.15 Valve types

The whole thing is expedited considerably if the tire and rim match rather generously. That is typically taken care of by selecting rims with a deep well, or rim bed (in preference to the box-section variety — see Fig. 7.8) and trying out the tire for fit. In fact, it is often possible to remove a tire by hand without the need for tire levers.

Tools and equipment:
tire repair kit, tire irons, tools to remove and reinstall wheel, sometimes spare tube

Procedure:
1.   Remove the wheel from the bike, holding back the chain by the rear derailleur (after having selected a gear that combines a small sprocket with a small chainring) if you're dealing with a rear wheel. If necessary to clear the brakes, either push the (limp) tire together locally, or release the brake cable.

2.   Check the valve: try to inflate and check whether air is escaping there. Sometimes a Schrader valve (see Fig. 7.15) will leak and can be fixed by screwing in the interior, using a narrow object, like a small screwdriver.

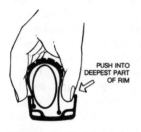

PUSH INTO
DEEPEST PART
OF RIM

7.16 Working tire into center of rim

3.   Check the circumference of the tire for visible signs of damage and mark their location, e.g. with a ball-point pen or by tying something around the nearest spoke.

4.   If the tire still contains air, push the pin of the valve in, for which the small round nut must be unscrewed on a Presta valve first.

5.   To loosen the tire, push one side of the tire towards the (deeper) center of the rim around the entire circumference of the wheel, as shown in Fig. 7.16, to loosen that side enough to ease removal.

6.   If it does not come off by hand, place the longer end of a tire lever under the side of the tire and hook the short end under a spoke, as shown in Fig. 7.17.

7.   Two or three spokes removed, do the same with the second tire lever.

8.   If necessary, insert the third tire lever two or three spokes in the opposite direction (if it is necessary and you have only two, remove one of the two installed and move it to the new location).

9.   Remove the tire levers and pull the rest of that side of the tire off by hand, working

7.17 Inserting tire levers

around, starting at the location of the tire levers.

10. Remove the tube from under the tire, pushing the valve out of the valve hole.

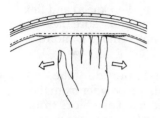

7.18 Removing bead from rim

11. Check the tube, starting at any location you may have marked as an obvious or probable cause of the puncture.

12. If the leak is not easily detected, inflate the tire and check carefully for escaping air, passing the tube by your eye, which is your most sensitive detection device. To date, I have not encountered a leak that could not be found this way, but it takes some practice.

13. If you are not able to detect escaping air, submerge the inflated tire in water (or, if not enough of that is available, rub a little water from your water bottle over the inflated tire, systematically working around and reinflating the tire as required to maintain adequate pressure.

14. Once you have established the location of the leak, mark it.

15. Take an appropriate patch from the patch kit (generally, the smallest size will do, except if you are dealing with several holes close together or with a long tear).

16. If necessary, dry the tube local to the leak. Roughen the area around the leak with sandpaper or scraper from the patch kit and wipe clean.

17. Take a sizeable drop of rubber solution from the tube in the patch kit and quickly spread it smoothly and evenly over an area around the leak that is a little larger than the patch.

18. Allow the rubber solution to dry one minute for a normal butyl tube (or twice that long if you should have a latex tube, recognized by its softness and its color: not black but white or red).

19. Remove the plastic or aluminum foil from the adhesive side of the patch without touching the adhesive, and quickly, yet accurately, place the patch on the area prepared, centered at the leak.

20. Push the patch down, then kneed and flex patch and tube together to make sure the patch adheres fully. If not, remove it and re-start at point 15.

21. Remove the foil on the outside of the patch, then sprinkle talcum powder from the patch kit — usually provided as a block from which you scrape some off — over the patch and the adhesive-coated area around it to prevent adhesion between the tube and the inside of the tire.

22. Inflate the tube partway to establish whether air escapes. If it does, there may be another hole or the first one was not patched properly. Fix or redo until the tube holds air.

23. After you have inflated the tube, while waiting to verify whether it holds air, check the inside of the tire to find and remove any embedded objects that may have caused the puncture — or cause subsequent ones. Particularly tricky in off-road cycling are thorns, which wear off to be invisible on the outside, yet protrude far enough inside to pinch the tube when the tire is compressed.

24. Also check inside the rim bed to make sure none of the spokes protrude and that they are covered by rim tape. File off any spokes that do protrude and replace or patch a defective rim tape.

25. When you are sure the problem is solved, let most of the air escape from the tube until it is limp but not quite empty.

26. Starting at the valve, put the tube back under the tire over the rim.

27. Starting opposite the valve and working in both directions towards it, pull the side of the

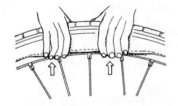

7.19 Pulling tire onto rim

tire back over the rim, making sure the tube does not get pinched between tire and rim.

28. If the tire has a Presta valve, reinstall the knurled locknut. Whatever the valve, make sure it is straight.

29. Inflate the tire partway and check once more to make sure the tube is not pinched, kneading the tire sidewalls from both sides, and making sure it is centered: the ridge on the side should be equally far from the rim around the circumference on both sides.

30. Inflate the tire to the desired pressure, preferably checking with a pressure gauge: 4–5 bar (60–75 psi) for smoothly paved roads, 2–3 bar (30–45 psi) for rough terrain, 1–1,5 bar (15–20 psi) for soft, loose soil, mud or snow.

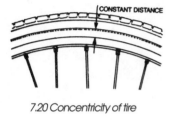

7.20 Concentricity of tire

Note: Even if you choose not to patch a tube while you are out in the field, replacing it with your spare tube instead, you should fix the puncture once you get home, so you can use the fixed tube as a spare — unless your spare time is worth more than $60 per hour (yes: at home, you can fix 10 tubes in one hour, at a price of at least $6 a piece).

Replacing Tube

If the puncture cannot be fixed, or if you want to install another tube for any other reason, proceed as described above for fixing a puncture up to step 10, then install the new tube and continue as described under steps 26 through 30.

Replacing Tire Casing

To replace the tire casing itself, initially also proceed as described above up to step 10 for fixing a tube. Then remove the other side of the tire in the same direction as the first side. Put one side of the new tire in place and continue as described in steps 26 through 30.

Patching Tire Casing

Sometimes a tire casing that is damaged can be repaired at least temporarily. To do that, proceed just as you did for the puncture repair. Fix the inside of the tire, using a 2.5 x 5 cm (1 x 2 in.) 'boot'. That can be a piece of canvas or a piece cut from the side of a discarded lightweight tire, first putting rubber solution on one side of this patch, allowing it to dry, and then reapplying rubber solution there *and* in the area of the tire where it has to be fixed. Generously sprinkle talcum powder over the area of the boot and around it to prevent the tire from sticking to the tube.

Chapter 8
The Drivetrain

The mountain bike's drivetrain comprises the parts that transmit the rider's legwork to the rear wheel: the bottom bracket with cranks and chainrings, the pedals, the chain, and the freewheel block with sprockets. The derailleurs, which are sometimes considered part of the drivetrain, will be covered separately in the next chapter, devoted to the gearing system.

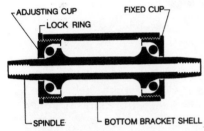

8.1 Adjustable (BSA) bottom bracket

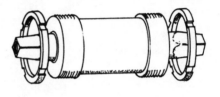

8.2 Cartridge bearing bottom bracket

The Bottom Bracket

This is the heart of the drivetrain, installed in the frame's bottom bracket shell. It comprises the spindle, or axle, to which the cranks are attached, and the ball bearings that allow it to turn smoothly. The two most common versions for mountain bike use are illustrated in Fig. 8.1 and 8.2, respectively. The BSA model, shown in Fig. 8.1, is the conventional adjustable type, whereas the cartridge (or sealed) unit, shown in Fig. 8.2, is not adjustable by the home mechanic.

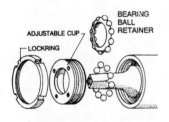

8.3 BSA bearing adjustment

Generally, if the cartridge bottom bracket develops play or tightness, it has to be replaced. Except for the Tioga and some other special models that are easily removable with common tools, overhauling a cartridge-type bottom bracket may require you to take the bike to a shop to have the work done fore you.

Adjusting BSA Bottom Bracket

Carry out this work on a BSA bottom bracket when the bearings have developed play or when they are too tight.

Tools and equipment:
bottom bracket wrenches

Procedure:
1. Loosen the lockring on the LH side by about one half turn.

2. Loosen the adjustable bearing cup by turning it ¼ turn counterclockwise if the bearing is too tight, clockwise if it is too loose.

3. Restraining the bearing cup, tighten the lockring, then readjust if necessary.

Notes:
1. Bottom bracket looseness is best detected with the cranks installed, using them for leverage while twisting sideways.

2. Tightness is best established when the cranks are removed, turning the spindle by hand.

3. If proper tools are not available, the adjustment can be carried out with the help of provisional tools: punch, drift and a hammer.

Overhauling Bottom Bracket

The description applies to BSA bottom brackets. Cartridge bearing bottom brackets vary from one model to the next and usually require special tools — refer any problems to the bike shop.

Tools and equipment:
bottom bracket tools, rags, solvent, bearing grease, crank tool

Disassembly procedure:
1. Remove the LH and RH cranks as described under *Replace Crank*.

2. Loosen and remove the lockring on the LH side.

3. Loosen and remove the adjustable bearing cup, catching the bearing balls, which are usually held in a retainer.

4. Pull the spindle out, also catching the balls on the other side.

Overhauling procedure:
1. Clean and inspect all parts, watching for corrosion, wear and damage, as evidenced by grooved or pitted bearing surfaces.

8.4 Bottom bracket tools

2. If there is serious damage or wear, also check the condition of the fixed (RH) bearing cup, which otherwise remains on the bike. On mountain bikes, it invariably has LH threading, meaning it is removed by turning clockwise, reinstalled by turning counterclockwise.

3. Replace any parts that are visibly corroded, damaged or worn, taking the old parts to the shop with you to make sure you get matching replacements.

Installation procedure:
1. Pack both cleaned bearing cups with bearing grease.

2. If the fixed bearing cup had been removed, reinstall it, turning it counterclockwise.

3. Push the bearing ball retainers in the grease-filled bearing cups, making sure they are such a way round that only the balls — not the metal of the retainer — contact the cup.

4. Put the spindle in from the LH side — with the longer end first if it is not symmetric, since that'll be where the RH crank with the chainrings is installed.

5. Install the adjustable cup with its bearing ball retainer in place.

6. Install the lockring.

7. Adjust the bearing as described in the preceding description until it runs smoothly and without play.

The Cranks

The mountain bike is invariably equipped with aluminum cotterless cranks. As shown in Fig. 8.6, these are held on the square tapered ends of the bottom bracket spindle by a matching square tapered hole and a bolt or nut (depending on the design of the spindle). Since the ones held with bolts are usually better than those held with nuts, choose the former type when replacing the bottom bracket.

The bolt or nut is covered by a dustcap, which protects the screw thread in the recess. This

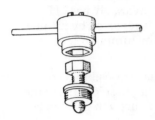

8.5 Crank extractor

screw thread is used to pull the crank off the spindle for maintenance or replacement by means of a crank extractor tool. The RH crank has an attachment spider or ring, to which the chainrings are bolted.

The first maintenance a new bike needs is the tightening of the cranks, since in the beginning the soft aluminum deforms so much that the connection between spindle and crank comes loose frequently until you have covered about 100–200 miles. This is the reason you should carry the wrench part of the crank tool in your repair kit. Beyond that, the crank is only removed when it is damaged or when you have to overhaul the bottom bracket. It is not uncommon in off-road cycling to bend a crank during a fall. Before you replace the entire crank, let a bike mechanic try to straighten it out. This requires a special tool that is not worth buying for the average home mechanic.

Replacing Crank

This job is necessary when a crank or an entire crankset has to be replaced. It also has to be done for some bottom bracket maintenance jobs.

Tools and equipment:
crank extractor, rag, grease or vaseline, sometimes Allen wrench

Removal procedure:
1. Remove the dustcap, which can generally be done with a coin, though some models require the use of an Allen key.

2. Unscrew the bolt or the nut with the wrench part of the crank tool, holding the crank firmly.

3. Remove the washer that lies under the bolt or the nut (this is an important step: if you forget to do this, you will not be able to remove the crank, damaging it instead).

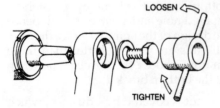

8.6 Removing or installing crank

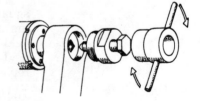

8.7 Pulling crank

4. Make sure the internal part of the crank extractor is retracted as far as it will go.

5. Screw the crank extractor into the threaded recess in the crank by at least three full turns — preferably more.

6. Holding the crank firmly with one hand, turn the handle of the crank extractor (or the wrench that fits on it instead of a handle on some models) in, which will eventually pull the crank off the spindle.

7. Remove the tool from the crank.

Installation procedure:
1. Clean the matching surfaces of the spindle and the crank hole, then apply a thin layer of lubricant to these surfaces.

2. Push the crank onto the spindle, making sure the two cranks are 180 degrees off-set and the crank with the attachment for the chainrings goes on the right.

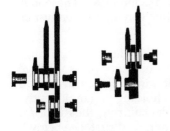

3. Install the washer.

8.8 Chainring attachment detail

4. Install the bolt or the nut and tighten it fully, then install the dustcap.

5. At about 25 mile intervals during the first 100–200 miles, firmly retighten the bolt or the nut.

The Chainrings

The three chainrings that are so characteristic for the mountain bike are installed on the RH crank by one of the methods shown in Fig. 8.8. Once a month, ascertain that the chainrings are still firmly in place by trying to tighten the little bolts that hold them to each other and to the cranks, respectively, countering on the other side.

Most chainrings are attached with Allen bolts, though some models use slotted nuts on one side, for which a slotted screwdriver or hooked wrench is used. The bigger chainring is sensitive to damage when it hits obstacles on the ground, and can be protected against exterior damage by installing a Rockring chainring guard, described in Chapter 11.

Chainring Wear and Damage

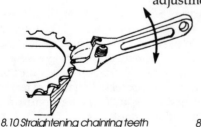

NEW TEETH   WORN TEETH

8.9 Chainring or sprocket wear

Chainring Replacement

The Pedals

Fig. 8.9 shows what happens if you allow the chainrings to wear too far. Eventually, that will result in increased resistance and poor shifting. Replace the chainrings if they are obviously worn or when teeth are cracked.

If individual teeth are bent, they can sometimes be straightened, using the procedure illustrated in Fig. 8.10. When the whole chainring is warped, it can be straightened by carefully using a wedge-shaped block of wood and pushing it between chainstay and chainring or between individual chainrings in the location where they are too close. These jobs can both be done while leaving the chainrings on the bike.

This job will be necessary when the chainrings are beyond repair or when you want to change to a different gearing range. To remove, undo the Allen bolts, while holding the crank steady. To replace the smaller chainring, the RH pedal generally has to be removed first (see below). In the case of Shimano Superglide (and the now virtually extinct off-round Bio-Pace) chainrings, make sure to match their orientation by means of the guide marker that should be lined up with the crankarm.

The mountain bike's pedals are inside no different from those installed on other bikes. A cross section is shown in Fig. 8.11. They are screwed into the cranks with a normal RH threaded connection on the right, a LH one on the left. Fig. 8.12 shows you how you can tell them apart, if they are not marked appropriately.

Pedal maintenance operations are limited to adjustment, overhauling and the replacement

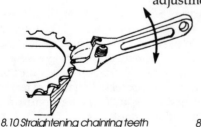

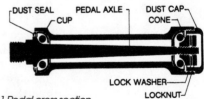

8.10 Straightening chainring teeth   *8.11 Pedal cross section*

of a pedal. There are special toeclips for installation on mountain bikes, covered in Chapter
11. Special clipless pedals will be discussed
separately below.

Replacing Pedal

This job may also be necessary when transporting the bike, e.g. on a plane or a bus. The
description is equally valid for regular and clipless pedals.

Tools and equipment:
Allen key or pedal wrench,
lubricant

Removal procedure:
1.   Restrain the crank firmly (e.g. with a rod
held horizontally just behind the crank and
over the top of the chainstays).

2.   Unscrew the connection between the pedal
and the crank. If the pedal has a hexagonal
recess in the end of the threaded stub
(reached from behind the crank), use the
Allen key. If not, use the open-ended wrench.

Note: Turn the LH pedal to the right (clockwise) to
unscrew, since it has LH screw thread.

Installation procedure:
1.   Clean the threaded hole in the crank and
the threaded stub on the pedal, then apply
some lubricant to both threaded surfaces.

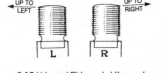

8.12 LH and RH pedal thread
detail

2.   Carefully align the screw thread and screw
in the pedal, making sure you turn the RH
pedal clockwise, the LH pedal counterclockwise.

Note: If you remove the pedals frequently, e.g. because you often travel with the bike on public
transportation, I suggest you place a thin
steel washer between the face of the crank
and the pedal stub. This will protect the
crank and the thread, making it much easier
to loosen and tighten the pedal.

Adjusting Pedal

Though some pedals have sealed cartridge
bearings that cannot be adjusted but must be
replaced when they develop play or resistance,
most pedals are built up as shown in the illustration Fig. 8.11. This type can easily be adjusted, referring to Fig. 8.13.

Tools and equipment:
dustcap wrench, wrench to fit locknut, small screwdriver

Procedure:
1. Remove the dustcap, using either pliers or a special dustcap wrench.

2. Loosen the locknut by one turn.

3. Lift the underlying keyed washer with the tip of the screwdriver to loosen it.

4. Using the screwdriver, turn the cone to the right (clockwise) to tighten the bearing, to the left (counterclockwise) to loosen it. Turn only ¼ turn at a time.

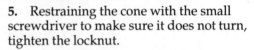

8.13 Pedal adjusting detail

5. Restraining the cone with the small screwdriver to make sure it does not turn, tighten the locknut.

6. Check and readjust if necessary: there should be neither noticeable play nor tightness.

7. Reinstall the dustcap.

Overhauling Regular Pedal

This is required if adjustment does not have the desired effect. Sometimes the problem will be a bent axle, and then — depending whether such parts are stocked for the model in question — you may have to replace the pedals altogether.

Tools and equipment:
dustcap wrench, wrench, small screwdriver

Disassembly procedure:
1. Remove the dustcap, using either pliers or a special dustcap wrench.

2. Loosen the locknut and remove it.

3. Lift the underlying keyed washer with the tip of the screwdriver to loosen it and then remove it.

4. Using the screwdriver, turn the cone to the left (counterclockwise) to loosen and remove it, catching the bearing balls as you do so.

5. Pull the pedal housing off the spindle or axle, also catching the bearing balls on the other side.

Overhauling procedure:
1. Clean and inspect all bearing surfaces and the pedal axle.

2. Replace anything that is damaged, corroded, grooved or pitted, as well as the pedal axle if it is bent — or the whole pedal if no spares are available.

Reassembly procedure:
1. Fill both bearing cups with grease and push the bearing balls in this bed of grease, making sure there is just a little room between: one less than the maximum that might seem to fit in a pinch. Be careful not to lose any balls at this stage.

2. Put the pedal housing on the axle with the larger side — the end without the dustcap screw threading — first (towards the crank)

3. After you've made sure you have not lost any bearing balls, install the adjustable cone.

4. Install the keyed washer with the projecting key fitting in the groove in the pedal axle.

5. Install the locknut, while restraining the cone with the small screwdriver to make sure it does not turn with it.

6. Adjust the bearing as described above.

7. Install the dustcap.

Clipless Pedals

Recently, clipless pedals have been introduced for mountain bikes, the most promising of which is the Shimano SPD. It requires the use of matching shoes, and the most important maintenance operation is exterior cleaning with water and a fine brush.

The clipless pedal can be replaced following the same instructions that apply to the regular pedal (see above). To overhaul or adjust the bearings, first remove the bearing cartridge with the special tool from the manufacturer, after which the cartridge can be maintained just like any regular pedal.

The Chain

The mountain bike is equipped with the same 3⁄32 x 1⁄2 in. chain used on most road bikes. Fig. 8.14 shows the construction of the chain. The life expectancy of a chain under off-road con-

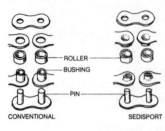

8.14 Chain construction details

ditions is limited to about six months — even less if you ride in mud, sand and dirt a lot.

Clean and Lubricate the chain as described in the section *Preventive Maintenance* in Chapter 3, at intervals that are consistent with the kind of weather and terrain you ride in. To do so, remove the chain to rinse it out in a solvent (e.g. kerosene) with 5—10% motor oil mixed in, and then lubricate it thoroughly. In the following section, we shall cover removal and installation of the chain.

Sometimes, when shifting problems occur after the bike has been in a spill, the reason will be a twisted chain. This may happen when the derailleur was twisted, trapping the chain in place. Check for this, and replace the chain if it is twisted.

When selecting a new chain, make sure you get one that is particularly narrow if your bike has eight sprockets in the back. I find that set-ups with Shimano Hyperglide freewheel and Superglide chainrings work just as well with other narrow chains as with the same manufacturer's special Hyperglide chain.

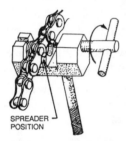

8.15 Use of chain rivet extractor

Replacing Chain

This has to be done whenever you replace it or remove it for a thorough cleaning job. Also some derailleur maintenance operations are best done with the chain removed from the bike. The Shimano Hyperglide chain, which is specially designed to match the same company's special tooth shape on the chainrings and sprockets requires special attention, that will be covered in a note at the end of the description.

Tools and equipment:
chain rivet extractor, rags

Removal procedure:
1.   With the aid of the derailleurs, and while turning the cranks with the rear wheel lifted off the ground, put the chain on the smallest chainring in the front and one of the smallest sprockets in the back.

2.   Put the chain rivet extractor on one of the pins between two links as shown in Fig. 8.15 with the punch firmed up against it.

3.   Turn in the handle by 6 turns, pushing the pin towards the opposite side.

4.   Turn the handle back until the tool can be removed.

5.   Try to separate the chain at this point, twisting it sideways. If it does not work, reinstall the tool and give it another turn until the chain comes apart. Just make sure the pin does not come out altogether, since that makes it very hard to reassemble the chain later.

Installation procedure:
1.   Make sure the derailleurs are set for the smallest chainring in the front and the second smallest or smallest sprocket in the back.

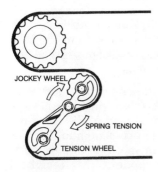

JOCKEY WHEEL

SPRING TENSION

TENSION WHEEL

8.16 Routing chain at rear derailleur

2.   Wrap the chain around the sprocket and the derailleur pulleys as shown in Fig. 8.16, also passing over the chainring and through the front derailleur cage.

3.   Routed this way, there should be just a little spring tension in the rear derailleur, tending to pull it tight.

4.   If the chain is too long, remove an *even* numbered set of links, following the same procedure as described above for removal of the chain, but pushing one pin out all the way.

5.   Using the chain rivet extractor from the side where the pin protrudes, push it back in until it projects equally far on both sides.

6. Twist the chain sideways a few times until it has come loose enough at this point to bend as freely as at the other links. If this can't be done, put the tool on the chain in the other slot (marked 'spreader position' in the illustration) and turn the handle against the pin just a little until the links are freed.

Note: If you should accidentally push the pin out all the way when disassembling, install a section of two new links instead, after removing the two last links on the end with the lost pin — taking care not to lose the pin this time.

Make sure you use a section of the same make and type of chain, since different chains make a poor match.

Hyperglide Note: The Shimano Hyperglide chain has one slightly oversize chain link pin that can be recognized because the link is black, and it should not be separated there. Split it anywhere else Instead, and remove the pin all the way, then replace it with a special, black link that is available with the chain or as a replacement from the bike shop. File off the pointed end of this special link before trying out the gears.

The Freewheel

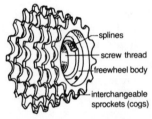

- splines
- screw thread
- freewheel body
- interchangeable sprockets (cogs)

8.17 Freewheel and sprockets

Most manufacturers use a freewheel block with six or seven sprockets (also called cogs) that is screwed on the screw thread of the rear hub. However, the so-called cassette-hub, such as the one made by Shimano, is becoming quite popular. On these models, the freewheel mechanism is integrated in the rear hub, while the sprockets are installed on it on splines and locked in place by means of a threaded ring or a threaded smallest sprocket.

As far as the guts of a freewheel mechanism are concerned, I shall not go into any detail here. If the freewheel doesn't work, get a new one (or a new hub, in the case of the cassette hub). What is more important is knowing how to lubricate the mechanism, how to exchange sprockets for those of a different size and how to remove a complete standard freewheel block. Those are the subjects that will be covered here.

Freewheel Lubrication

Do this job if the freewheel is running roughly, yet is not so old that it seems reasonable to replace it (do that after about a year's heavy use).

Tools and equipment:
SAE 40 or thicker oil, cleaning materials, old can or similar receptacle

Procedure:

1. Before you lubricate the mechanism, clean the sprockets, the spaces between them and the visible end of the freewheel block, preferably with the wheel removed from the bike.

2. On freewheels with an oil hole, enter oil through it until it oozes out at the end.

8.18 Freewheel lubrication

3.   On freewheels without an oil hole, put the wheel on its side, the freewheel facing up, with a receptacle under the hub to catch excess oil. Turn the freewheel relative to the wheel, and enter oil through the gap that is visible between stationary and turning parts of the freewheel mechanism — until it comes out clean on the other side.

4.   Let drip until no more oil comes out, then clean off excess oil.

Freewheel Replacement

This job must often be carried out if a spoke on the RH side of the rear wheel has to be replaced. The freewheel and the sprockets also wear, and about once a season it will make sense to replace the whole freewheel block.

There are two types of freewheel in use on mountain bikes: separate units screwed on to the outside of the hub and cassette type freewheels that actually contain the RH wheel bearing.

Replacing Screwed-On Freewheel

If your freewheel does not say anything like Freehub or cassette, you will most likely have this regular screwed-on model. Once the wheel is removed from the wheel, you can usually tell, because on these models there will be internal splines or notches into which a freewheel removal tool fits.

Tools and equipment:
freewheel tool, wrench or vice

Removal procedure:
1.   Remove the rear wheel from the bike, following the instructions in Chapter 7.

2.   Remove the quick-release or the axle nut and its washer on the RH side.

3.   Place the freewheel tool on the freewheel with the ribs or prongs on the tool exactly matching the splines or notches in the freewheel body.

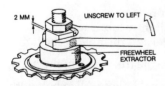

8.19 Screwed-on freewheel removal

4.   Install the quick-release or the RH axle nut, leaving about 2 mm (3⁄32 in.) space between tool and nut.

5.   If you have a vice available, clamp the tool in with the side matching the freewheel facing up; if not, place the wrench on the flat

faces of the tool and clamp the wheel securely, e.g. with the tire pushed against the floor and one wall of the room.

6. Turning counterclockwise to loosen the screw thread between hub and freewheel, forcefully turn either the wheel relative to the vice, or the wrench relative to the wheel — about one turn, until the space between the tool and the nut is taken up.

7. Loosen the nut another two turns and repeat this process until the freewheel can be removed by hand, holding the tool.

Installation procedure:
1. Clean the threaded surfaces of the freewheel (inside) and the hub (outside), and coat these surfaces with lubricant to prevent corrosion and to ease subsequent removal.

2. Put the wheel down horizontally with the threaded end facing up.

3. Carefully screw the freewheel on by hand until it cannot be tightened further that way.

4. Install the wheel, and allow the driving force to 'automatically' tighten it as you ride.

Replacing cassette Freewheel

Tools and equipment:
9 or 10 mm Allen key
(depending on make)

If no internal notches or splines to take a tool are visible, you probably have a cassette type freewheel. It is held inside the rear hub with an internal hollow Allen bolt.

Removal procedure
1. Disassemble the hub bearing on one side and remove the axle.

2. Hold the wheel firmly and unscrew the freewheel off with the big Allen key (10 mm for Shimano, 9 mm for SunTour and Campagnolo.

Installation procedure:
1. Clean and very lightly lubricate the surfaces of the freewheel and the hole in the hub.

2. Accurately place the freewheel in the hub.

3. Tighten the internal hollow Allen bolt with the big Allen key.

8.20 Construction of cassette hub with freewheel and

Replacing Sprocket of Cassette Freewheel

On these units, the sprockets are held in splines on the freewheel body, held together with a lockring (Shimano) or a screwed-on smallest sprocket (SunTour and Campagnolo).

On Shimano Hyperglide sprockets, which owe their easy shifting to subtle alignment of specially shaped teeth, one of the splines is wider, so make sure you line them up properly.

Tools and equipment:
one or two chain whips, for Shimano: freewheel tool

Disassembly procedure:
1.   Remove the wheel from the bike following the appropriate description in Chapter 7.

2.   Place the wheel horizontally in front of you with the freewheel facing up.

3.   Using the appropriate tool, remove the last sprocket or the notched ring holding together the sprockets.

4.   Remove the sprockets and the spacers that lie on the splined end that is connected to the rest of the hub and contains the built-in freewheel mechanism, marking the sequence of the various sprockets and spacers.

Installation procedure:
1.   Clean all parts and grease them lightly.

2.   Install the sprockets and the spacers in the same sequence.

3.   Screw on the last sprocket or the notched ring, while countering with a chain whip wrapped around one of the other sprockets, or on Shimano models using the freewheel tool.

4.   Reinstall the wheel.

**Replacing Sprocket of
Screwed-On Freewheel**

On these units, the sprockets are generally either all or partly screwed onto the freewheel. The procedure is similar to that outlined for the cassette freewheel, except that you will need two chain whips — one wrapped around the smallest sprocket, one around one of the other ones. When you have finished reassembly, put the chain on the smallest sprocket and stand on the pedals to tighten it.

**New Drivetrain
Developments**

In recent years, several new drivetrain components have been introduced. In addition to the new SunTour, Campagnolo and Shimano units based on smaller chainrings (42 teeth for the largest chainring, rather than 46 or 48 as is customary), the major novelty is Shimano's new lightweight cassette freewheel hub. Here the largest sprockets are sitting on a stepped spider and are held individually. To replace them, unscrew the lockring and the smaller sprockets first.

Chapter 9
The Gearing System

The mountain bike's derailleur gearing system is depicted in Fig. 9.1. It comprises a front derailleur, also called changer, and a rear derailleur, both operated by means of thumb shifters mounted on the handlebars and connected to the derailleurs by means of flexible Bowden cables. The rear derailleur moves the chain sideways from one sprocket, or cog, to another on a freewheel block mounted on the rear wheel, while the front derailleur moves the chain sideways from one chainring to another.

System Overview

Since the various sprockets and chainrings have different numbers of teeth, varying the combination achieves a lower or higher gear. A low gear is achieved by selecting a small chainring in the front and a big sprocket in the rear. A high gear results when a large chainring is combined with a small sprocket.

Nowadays, all mountain bikes come equipped with indexed gearing. That means that there are distinct stops on the shift levers for each of the gears, eliminating the need for fidgety adjustments when shifting. There are two major types of shift levers, mounted on top of and under the handlebars respectively, the former being the experts' choice and

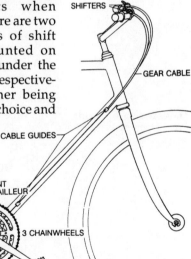

9.1 The derailleur system

SHIFTERS

GEAR CABLE

CABLE GUIDES

FREEWHEEL WITH SPROCKETS

FRONT DERAILLEUR

3 CHAINWHEELS

REAR DERAILLEUR

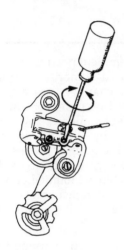

9.2 Adjusting set-stop screws

Adjusting Derailleur Range

Tools and equipment:
small screwdriver, often a rag

the latter typically used on novice bikes. Shimano's latest versions of under-the-bar shifters now have the return lever sticking out to the front, whereas on other models the two levers are mounted above each other on the rider's side of the handlebars. Functionally, there is not much difference.

This chapter will describe all maintenance operations necessary to maintain and adjust the gearing system and its individual components. For maintenance of the sprockets and chainrings, you are referred to the preceding Chapter 8, which is devoted to the drivetrain.

Although several manufacturers claim universal suitability of their equipment with most other makes and models of other components, this is generally true only for perfectly adjusted and unworn components. In practice, it will probably be better to have a shifter from the same manufacturer as the derailleur, which in turn will work best on a matching freewheel.

The most frequently occurring derailleur problem requiring maintenance is that one of the derailleurs either exceeds or fails to reach its full range. In that case, the chain is shifted sideways but either drops off the innermost or outermost chainring or sprocket, or fails to reach it. The former is the more frustrating, since it stops motion, as the chain drops off by the side of the last chainring or sprocket, while in the latter case the extreme gear just cannot be reached. It is easy enough to correct either of these problems.

Procedure:
1.   Establish just what the nature of your problem is:

☐   front or rear derailleur;

☐   too far or not far enough;

☐   left or right.

2.   If necessary, put the chain back on chainring or sprocket.

3. Observe how each derailleur is equipped with two set-stop screws, as shown in Fig 9.2, usually equipped with a little spring under the head, and usually marked with an H and an L for high and low gear, respectively.

4. Tightening one of these screws limits the range of the derailleur in the corresponding direction, while loosening the screw expands it.

5. If e.g. the chain came off on the RH side (outside, or high gear) on the front, tighten the screw marked H of the front derailleur by perhaps one turn. If it did not quite reach the last gear on that side, loosen the screw by about that much.

6. Check all the gears, turning the cranks with the rear wheel lifted off the ground. Readjust as necessary.

Note: If problems persist, adjust the relevant derailleur system completely, as described for front and rear derailleurs separately below.

The Rear Derailleur

Fig. 9.3 shows a typical rear derailleur as used on a mountain bike. Almost to the exclusion of all others, indexed mechanisms are used on mountain bikes, generally set up to select one of usually 7 (sometimes 8, older models sometimes only 5 or 6) sprockets. The thumb shifter has a ratchet device that corresponds with specific settings of the rear derailleur, which in turn correspond with the positions of the individual sprockets.

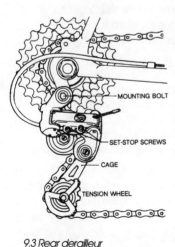

9.3 Rear derailleur

In the case of top-mounted shifters, there is usually a small selection lever (or sometimes a knob) to switch from the indexed mode to the so-called friction mode (actually just a finer ratchet), which allows the selection of intermediate positions. This is sometimes of benefit when the mechanism is no longer adjusted properly, allowing the selection of the right gear — even if that is at the expense of more fidgety shifting. On the road, or in the terrain, this will be your quick solution to any gearing problems that develop, since exact adjustment is more easily carried out at home. The index and friction modes are usually identified by the letters I and F, respectively, marked on the shifter.

Adjusting Rear Derailleur

Most gearing problems can be eliminated by some form of derailleur adjustment. This job will be described in great detail in the following procedures.

Tools and equipment:
small screwdriver, sometimes wrench to fit cable clamp bolt

Procedure:
1. To get by until you have time to do a more thorough adjusting job, select the friction mode (letter F) on the RH shifter and continue riding. This is also the first step when you want to adjust the derailleur properly.

2. To adjust the derailleur, first carry out the adjustment as described above under *Adjusting Derailleur Range.*

3. If the gears still do not engage properly, adjust the cable tension, using the built-in adjusting barrel shown in Fig 9.4.

4. Set the derailleur in the position for the outside (small) sprocket, lifting the rear wheel and turning the cranks for this and all subsequently described gear changes while adjusting, until the chain engages that gear (or the one next to it, if this can't be achieved).

5. Holding the adjusting barrel, loosen the locknut, then tighten or loosen the barrel to either release or increase tension on the cable.

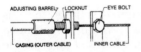

9.4 Cable adjusting detail

6. If the range of the adjusting barrel is inadequate, the cable must be clamped in at a different point: screw the adjusting barrel in all the way, loosen the eye bolt or clamp nut that holds the cable at the derailleur, pull the cable taut (but not under tension) from the end, and tighten the clamp nut or eye bolt again.

7. Try out all the gears and readjust the range if that should be necessary, following the description above.

8. Now the derailleur operates correctly in friction mode. The next step will be to fine-tune

the indexing. To do that, first with the shifter still set in the F position, select the lowest gear (biggest sprocket in the rear, combined with smallest chainring in the front) and make sure it achieves this gear correctly.

9. Select the highest gear again (largest chainring, smallest sprocket), then put the shifter in index mode, marked with the letter I.

10. Adjust the cable tension until the chain runs smoothly without scraping against the derailleur cage or the next larger sprocket.

11. Move the shifter one notch for the next lower gear in the back, engaging the second smallest sprocket if it is adjusted correctly.

12. If the derailleur does not move the chain to the next sprocket, tighten the cable by about one half revolution of the adjusting barrel.

13. If the derailleur shifts past this second smallest sprocket, loosen the cable tension with the adjusting barrel by about half a turn.

14. Repeat steps 10 through 13 until the mechanism works smoothly in these two gears.

15. With the derailleur set for the second smallest sprocket, tighten the cable with the adjusting barrel just so far that the chain runs noisily, scraping against the third smallest sprocket.

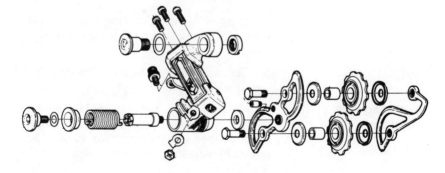

9.5 Construction of rear derailleur

16. Loosen the cable tension just so far that the noises subdue to achieve the optimal setting.

17. Verify that the derailleur selects all gears with the shifter set in the appropriate position and readjust if necessary.

Notes: **1.** If adjusting does not solve the problem, first replace the cable. Replace the shifter if this does not lick the problem either.

2. Most rear derailleurs have a third adjusting screw, with which the angle of the mechanism can be varied. Select the gear in which the chain runs on the biggest sprocket, and adjust it so that the chain comes close to it, without the sprocket scraping the pulley.

Overhauling Rear Derailleur

This work will be necessary when so much dirt has built up that operation of the mechanism has become unreliable and can not be solved by adjusting. Fig. 9.5 shows a typical derailleur and the parts that can be removed easily for this work.

Tools and equipment:
wrench to fit bolts through guide wheel and tension wheel, solvent, rags, lubricants

Procedure:
1. Remove the bolts at the little wheels, or pulleys, over which the chain runs, catching the wheels and the various other parts.

2. Clean the wheels and the bushings inside, as well as all other parts of the mechanism that are more easily accessible now.

3. Lubricate the bushings in the wheels with grease or vaseline and all pivots with light spraycan oil

4. Reassemble the chain cage with the little wheels, guiding the chain as shown in Fig. 9.6.

5. Try out all the gears and adjust the derailleur if necessary.

Replacing Rear Derailleur

This is done when you overhaul the bike completely and when the derailleur must be replaced because its operation cannot be restored by adjusting or overhauling.

Tools and Equipment:
wrench (or chain rivet
extractor), Allen key, small
screwdriver, rag

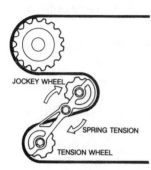

9.6 Routing of chain at derailleur

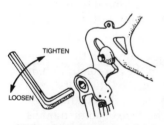

9.7 Derailleur attachment detail

The Front Derailleur

Adjusting Front Derailleur

Removal procedure:
1. If you prefer to leave the chain intact, remove the bolts at the little wheels over which the chain runs, catching the wheels and the other parts.

2. Otherwise, separate the chain, as described in the Chapter 8.

3. Undo the cable attachment and catch the pieces of cable casing.

4. Undo the derailleur attachment bolt (see Fig. 9.7) and remove the derailleur.

Installation procedure:
1. When you get a new derailleur, make sure that it is compatible with the shifter and the freewheel block installed on the bike.

2. Put the new derailleur in the same position as the old one was (see Fig. 9.7), checking to make sure it pivots freely around the attachment bolt.

3. Attach the cable.

4. Either install the chain (if it had been removed) or open up the cage at the guide wheel in the cage to put the chain in place, then reinstall the guide wheel. The chain must be routed as shown in Fig. 9.6.

5. Try out all the gears and adjust the derailleur and the cable tension if necessary.

Fig. 9.8 illustrates a typical front derailleur. Though most front derailleurs are also indexed, requiring a matching indexed shifter in the front, many mountain bikes are still equipped with non-indexed models, which seem to be quite acceptable to most people.

The major maintenance work on the front derailleur is the range adjusting procedure described above. In addition, the cable tension can be adjusted similarly to that for the rear derailleur if it does not shift properly.

This job must be done when the front derailleur 'dumps' the chain by the side of the chainrings or when one chainring cannot be reached.

Tools and equipment:
small screwdriver, wrench
to fit cable clamp bolt

Procedure:

1. First carry out any adjustment of the set-stop screws that may be necessary, following the description *Adjust Derailleur Range* above.

2. Set the shifter in the position for the highest gear with the chain on the large outside chainring.

3. In this position, the cable should be just taut, though not under tension.

4. If necessary, tension or loosen it by clamping the cable in at a different point: loosen the eye bolt or clamp nut, pull the cable taut and tighten the eye bolt or clamp nut again.

5. Check all gears and make any other adjustments that may be necessary.

Replacing Front Derailleur

This may become necessary if the mechanism is bent or damaged — usually the result of a fall.

Tools and equipment:
Allen key, wrench, small
screwdriver, chain rivet
extractor

Removal procedure:

1. Loosen the cable attachment by unscrewing the eye bolt or the clamp nut, and pull the cable end out.

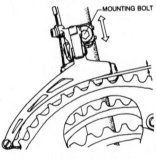

MOUNTING BOLT

9.8 Front derailleur installation

2. Either remove the chain with the chain rivet extractor or open up the derailleur's chain guide cage by removing the little bolt through the bushing that connects the two sides in the back of the cage of some models.

3. Undo the attachment bolt.

Installation procedure:

1. Install the derailleur on the seat tube, above the chainrings and with the cage parallel to the chainrings. Don't tighten it solidly yet.

2. Fine-tune the position, leaving a distance of 2–4 mm (3/32–3/16 in.) clearance between the largest chainring and the bottom of the cage, making sure it is aligned. Now tighten the attachment bolt fully.

3. Feed the cable through the mechanism as shown, and attach it in the eye bolt or under the clamp nut.

4. Adjust the cable tension so that it is just taut, but not under tension, with the shifter set for the highest gear and the chain on the largest chainring.

5. Check all the gears and adjust the derailleur range if necessary.

The Shifters

9.9 Top-mounted shifter

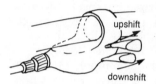

9.10 One-sided under-the-bar shifter

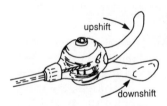

9.11 Two-sided under-the-bar shifter

Replacing Shifter

Tools and equipment:
screwdriver, wrench

Fig. 9.9 shows a typical indexed top-mounted, or over-the-bar, shifter, while fig. 9.10 and 9.11 depict two versions of under-the-bar shifters, the one per 9.11 being installed on many newer bikes. In addition, there are so-called wishbone shifters that are mounted under the handlebars, but work on the same principle as top-mounted shifters

Whatever the type, if it does not give satisfactory service, as evidenced by the derailleur's jumping out of the selected gear, the reason may be a damaged or corroded derailleur cable. So first check it, and replace it if necessary.

If the cable and the derailleur themselves are working properly, the problem may be due to either insufficient tension on the spring inside the mechanism, to dirt or corrosion, or to wear of the notched ring inside. Only in the latter case will it be necessary to replace the shifter.

First try cleaning and tensioning the shifter. Take it apart carefully and note where the various bits and pieces go. Then clean and lightly lubricate all parts. Finally reassemble and if necessary turn the screw that holds it all together a little tighter.

If the shifter cannot be made to work by means of adjustment and cable replacement, the whole unit can easily be replaced, as described here.

Removal procedure:
1. Undo the cable at the derailleur.

2. Remove the shifter attachment screw.

3. Pull the cable out and catch the cable casing and any loose items.

Installation procedure:
1. Attach the shifter in the desired location.

2. Feed the cable through the shifter with the nipple in the recess as shown in Fig. 9.12.

3. Guide the cable through the various guides and the cable casing, and attach the end at the derailleur.

4. Adjust the derailleur cable tension as described separately for front and rear derailleurs above.

Gear Cable

For indexed shifters, relatively stiff stainless steel inner cables and a nylon sleeve between inner cable and cable casing were introduced. These same cables can of course also be used on non-indexed systems. They only need to be cleaned from time to time and checked to make sure they are not pinched or damaged anywhere. Other cables (without the nylon sleeve) must also be lubricated from time to time. This is best done by removing them and smearing grease or vaseline over the inner cable. Alternatively, squirt a few drops of oil between the inner cable and the cable casing at the ends where the inner cable disappears in the casing.

Replacing Derailleur Cable

This work is necessary if the cable is pinched or otherwise damaged, or if the inner cable shows signs of corrosion or frayed strands. Especially for use with under-the-bar shifters, the cable must match the shifter, since the two major manufacturers (Shimano and SunTour) use different nipple shapes.

Tools and equipment:
screwdriver, wrench to fit cable clamp bolt

Removal procedure:
1. Undo the cable at the derailleur by loosening the cable clamp nut or the eye bolt that holds the cable to the derailleur.

2. Put the shifter in the position for the highest gear.

3. On under-the-bar shifters, open up the mechanism only to the point where the cable and the nipple are exposed.

4. Push the cable free at the shifter.

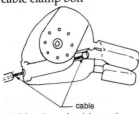

9.12 Seating of cable and nipple in shifter

5. Pull the cable out and catch the cable casing and any other loose items.

Installation procedure:
1. Feed the cable through the shifter as shown in Fig. 9.12 with the nipple in the recess. On a SunTour under-the-bar shifter, pay attention to the orientation of the eccentric nipple.

2. Guide the cable through the various guides and the cable casing, and attach the end at the derailleur.

3. Adjust the derailleur cable tension as described separately for front and rear derailleurs.

New Developments

Although the modern index derailleur system is a big improvement over the conventional systems common only a few years ago, development of the mountain bike's gearing is likely to continue. Each year some improvement is introduced. Some of the most recent innovations include twist-grip shifters, available from Campagnolo, Grip-Shift and Sachs.

Only a few years ago, one of the most promising of these seemed to be the Browning front shifter licensed by SunTour. In this system the chainrings have hinged sections that are moved over to pick up and deposit the chain to the next bigger or smaller chainring. However, at about the same time, Shimano's Hyperglide chainrings were refined to the point that front shifts now work just as smoothly with a regular front derailleur — at a much lower price. Most recently, the French Mavic company introduced an electronically controlled shifting system, but it is my guess manual operation will remain the more common solution

Of course, this is not the last word either, and you can expect to see new gearing developments cropping up from time to time. Mostly, a little common sense and the experience gained by working on other parts of the bike will help you with any maintenance problems on those items, if the manufacturer's literature doesn't show you the way.

Chapter 10
The Brakes

Figures 10.1 through 10.3 show the three types of brakes used most frequently on mountain bikes. All are mounted on bosses that are brazed or welded on the front fork in the front and either the chain stays or the seat stays in the rear. In the rear, cantilever brakes are always installed on the seat stays, the roller-cam and the U-brake sometimes underneath the chain stays, although these can also be installed on the seat stays — providing the bosses are in the appropriate location.

Brake Types

In addition to the types shown, there are several special models available for mountain bike use, including hydraulically operated brakes. Since these are not only very uncommon but also still in their infancy, at least in the form as used on mountain bikes, I have not included specific instructions for their maintenance, referring you instead to the information provided by the manufacturer, which can be obtained through the shop that sold you the bike — or the brake, if it is subsequently installed.

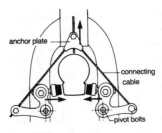

All of the more common mountain bike brakes are connected to the hand lever by means of a flexible Bowden cable. Usually, the LH lever controls the front brake, while the RH lever operates the one in the rear, though they could be reversed.

In many cases, the cable for the front brake runs either over a roller mounted under the handlebar stem or through a hole in the stem. Both solutions are a bit of a pain, since they require a full brake readjustment whenever the handlebar position has been changed. It is better to install an anchor that is either clamped between the lock washer and the locknut of the headset or around the stem above the head set.

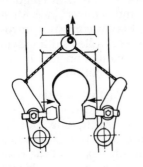

10.1 Conventional (top) and low-profile (bottom) cantilever brakes

Cantilever and U-brakes have a connecting cable between the two sides. This cable must be kept as short as possible (top angle of cable

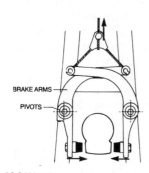

10.2 U-brake

triangle as big as possible) if the two sides are to be pushed together enough for adequate brake force. Recently, low-profile cantilever brakes have become popular, which do not protrude as far as conventional models. Shimano's versions don't have a conventional straddle cable: instead, the main cable runs to one of the brake arms and the second brake arm is connected to it via a short cable and an connecting clamp. They only work well if adjusted using the manufacturer's adjusting gauge for the model in question.

The most frequently required brake maintenance operation is cleaning the rim: greasy rims are the most common cause of poor braking. I'll also cover adjustment and replacing of brake cable and brake pads, and centering the brake. The latter operation brings both brake pads (on either side) equally far from the rim. Finally, I shall cover overhauling or replacement work of brakes and levers.

General Brake Check

Whatever type of brake, check its effectiveness from time to time to make sure it won't let you down. First pull each lever with the bike standing still, making sure each brake firmly engages when about 2 cm (¾ in.) of space remains between the brake lever and the handlebars.

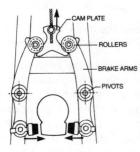

10.3 Cam-operated brake

Next, riding at walking speed, apply the rear brake fully. It should be possible to block the rear wheel, resulting in skidding. Then do the same with the front brake. In this case, the braking effect should be strong enough to make the bike tip forward if you are leaning forward on the handlebars — release the brake if it does.

If either of these criteria is not satisfied, adjust the brake according to the specific instructions for the type of brake in question. But before you do, check whether the brake pads touch the rim over their full width, as shown in Fig. 10.4, when the lever is applied. If it does not, adjust the brake pads (also called brake blocks or brake shoes), following the description below.

Adjusting or Replacing Brake Pads

If the brake pads do not lie flat on the side of the rim over their full width and length when the lever is engaged fully, they should be repositioned. Note that there are two general types of brake pad attachment: bolt mounted and stud mounted. In the latter case, the brake pad is not held in the brake arm directly, but it has a stud that in turn is clamped in an eye bolt on the brake arm.

Tools and equipment:
wrench to fit brake shoe attachment bolt

Procedure:

1.   Loosen the bolt that holds the brake pad to the brake arm by about one turn.

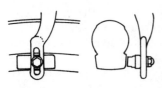

10.4 Brake pad position on rim

2.   While applying the corresponding brake lever with modest hand force, move the brake pads in the position illustrated in Fig. 10.4, then increase lever force. You may have to twist the brake shoe and the underlying spherical and cupped washers shown in Fig. 10.5 — or whatever other device is provided for angular adjustment — to achieve this position. Toeing-in is the word used to describe the situation whereby the front of the brake pad hits the rim before the rest does, and it is done to prevent vibrations and squealing.

10.5 Brake pad alignment with conical washers

3.   Pushing the brake pad against the side of the rim firmly with one hand, while at the same time making sure it does not shift from its correct position, tighten the bolt fully.

4.   Check to make sure the brake works correctly, and fine-tune the adjustment if necessary.

Adjusting Brake

The most common type of brake adjustment is that required to tighten the cable a little in order to compensate for brake pad wear. This operation is about the same, whatever type of brake you have. First carry out the brake pad adjustment mentioned above, though. If you don't, there is a risk of the brake shoe sooner or later slipping off the side of the rim, hitting either the tire (on U-brake or roller-cam brake) or the spokes (on a cantilever brake).

10.6 Cable attachment detail

Tools and equipment:
sometimes wrenches to fit cable clamp bolt

Procedure:

1.   Loosen the tension on the cable. Though some brakes have a special quick-release at the lever or somewhere else, it is generally

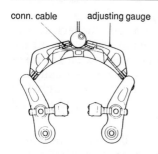

conn. cable   adjusting gauge

10.7 Low profile cantilever brake adjusting detail

done by squeezing the brake arms against the rim and unhooking either the connecting cable (U-brake or cantilever brake) or the cam plate (roller-cam brake).

2. To increase cable tension, adjust the cable adjuster (usually installed at the brake lever): loosen the locknut, screw the barrel adjuster out, and finally retighten the locknut, while holding the barrel adjuster.

3. Check operation of the brake, and fine-tune the adjustment if necessary.

Note: If the adjusting range is inadequate, clamp in the cable at a different point at the brake (Fig. 10.6), after first screwing in the barrel adjuster all the way. Finally use the barrel adjuster to fine-tune.

Note on Low-Profile Brakes: On Shimano low-profile cantilever brakes, the adjustment requires the use of the manufacturer's tool (actually just a plastic gauge) for the model in question, following Fig. 10.7. Put the tool in place, attach the main cable, and finally the connecting cable.

Centering Cantilever Brake

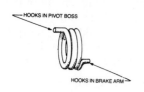

HOOKS IN PIVOT BOSS

HOOKS IN BRAKE ARM

10.8 Cantilever return spring

This work is necessary if one brake shoe is markedly closer to the side of the rim than the other, though the wheel is properly centered. First try adjusting the position of the pad in the brake arm. Most newer models have a limit screw in one of the brake arms that is screwed in or out to achieve the desired effect. If that does not solve the problem, remove the mounting bolts and place the end of one of the spring (Fig. 10.8) in a different hole in the pivot boss. If there is only one hole, bend the spring in the appropriate direction using two pairs of pliers. Reassemble and repeat if necessary.

Centering U-Brake

The U-brake is centered by means of a tiny Allen screw installed vertically down just below one of the brake pivots. Tighten or loosen this screw by one or two turns to bring the brake arm on the same side closer to or further from the side of the rim.

Be particularly careful to adjust the brake pads close enough to the rim to assure they contact the rim fully when applied. On a cantilever brake, brake pad wear left unchecked will eventually cause the brake pad to slip off the rim and hit the spokes, whereas on U-brakes and roller-cam brakes they will eventually rub on the tire sidewall, which — though less dangerous — causes tire wear instead of good braking performance.

Roller-Cam Brake

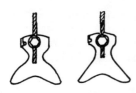

10.9 Roller cam cam plate types

This brake is more generally used in the rear of mountain bikes than it is in the front, since in this location its advantage of narrow width is most evident. There are two basic versions of this brake on the market: with straight-sided triangular cam plate and with curved-sided cam plate as shown in Fig. 10.9.

The latter is designed to provide progressively increasing brake force (and progressively decreasing travel) as the lever is pulled further and the brake pads come closer to the rim. The straight-sided model, on the other hand, is less sensitive to improper adjustment and is therefore preferred for use on low-cost mountain bikes. The other point to watch on these brakes is that most have a threaded brake pad mounting stud, which is clamped into the mount on the brake arm by means of an Allen-bolt.

Adjusting Roller-Cam Brake

Carry out this procedure whenever the brake does not seem to be operating properly. Before you do, carry out the two following simple checks, since they reveal the problems that are often the cause and are easy enough to correct:

1.   Make sure the rim is clean: sometimes it is merely a matter of a greasy and slippery rim.

2.   Check and, if necessary, correct the cable tension in such a way that the brake is applied fully while the brake lever is still at least 2 cm (¾ in.) away from the handlebars at its closest point. If not, readjust, following the instruction *Adjust Brake Cable*.

Note: If the problem cannot be solved as described above, proceed to the adjusting instruction.

Tools and equipment:
Allen key, wrench, cone
wrench

Procedure:
1.   Check the alignment of the brake pads on
the rim: they must lie flat and fully contact
the side of the rim when the lever is pulled. If
not, adjust.

2.. Check whether the brake pads protrude
the right distance from the brake arm: First
measure the distance between the brake arm
mounting pivots (dimension A in Fig. 10.10)
and determine the correct protrusion (dimension B) according to the following table:

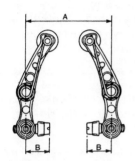

Dimension A	Dimension B
92 mm	29 mm
90 mm	28 mm
88 mm	27 mm
86 mm	26 mm
84 mm	25 mm

*10.10 Definitions for use with roller
cam brake table*

If the dimensions do not match, adjust until
they do.

3.   To adjust the alignment of the brake pads,
unscrew the fixing bolt by two turns, turn
and twist the brake pad stud in or out in such
a way that the brake pad contacts the rim
properly, hold it in position (preferably while
someone keeps the lever pulled), and tighten
the fixing bolt.

4.   Fine-tune the adjustment to provide 1 mm
(1/32 in.) of toe-in, meaning the front of the
brake pad should touch the rim just before the
rear portion does. To do this, loosen the brake
shoe fixing bolt, raise the rear part off the rim
a little, while ascertaining that the front portion still touches, then tighten the nut at the
back of the fixing bolt, while holding the front
by means of a 5 mm Allen key and making
sure the brake pad does not twist.

*10.11 Spreading roller cam
brake arms*

5.   Check the centering of the brake pads, after
first making sure the rim itself is centered between the frame stays (or fork blades, in case
the brake is used in the front) and correcting
if necessary. If the distance between the side
of the rim and the brake pad is different on
both sides, adjust.

6. The centering of the brake is a function of the spring tension, and most models have two separate springs that can be adjusted individually. To do this, first check to make sure the fixing nuts on the brake arm pivot bolts are tight, then use a 15 mm cone wrench (or any flat open-ended wrench of this size) to turn the pivot bushings immediately under the brake arms by only a very slight angular amount, until the two brake arms are centered relative to the rim.

7. Sometimes it is necessary to readjust the brake pad location, following steps 3–4 above, after this operation, so the brake pads are the same distance and touch the rim correctly.

Brake Overhauling or Replacement

Though rarely done, this work is recommended once a year or whenever the brake gives unsatisfactory performance and adjustment does not solve the problem.

Although there are slight differences between the procedure as it applies to different brakes, you will find a general description here, including comments for specific models. Most comments apply to all brakes, though.

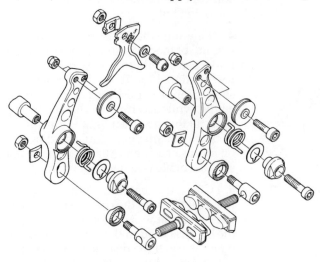

10.12 Roller-cam brake construction

This work is most easily carried out while the wheel is removed. For easy wheel removal, push the brake pads together just enough to unhook the cable (U-brake or cantilever). On the roller-cam, remove the cam plate, then loosen the tip of one spring and spread the brake arms asymmetrically, as shown in Fig. 10.11.

Tools and equipment: cone wrench or other flat open-ended wrench, Allen key, wrench, needle-nose pliers

Removal procedure:

1.   Pull the brake arms together at the brake pads and release the cable — on the roller cam-brake by twisting the cam plate out from between the rollers.

2.   Check the condition of the cable and replace it if necessary: remove the cable anchor clamp using a wrench on the nut and an Allen key on the bolt part. Pull the cable out, and later insert the new one. If an end cap is installed on the end of the cable, it must be pulled off with e.g. needle-nose pliers — I recommend soldering the end of the cable to prevent fraying, following the instructions under *Replacing Brake Cable*.

3.   Unscrew the fixing nut or bolt on top of the brake arm pivot bolt of each brake arm.

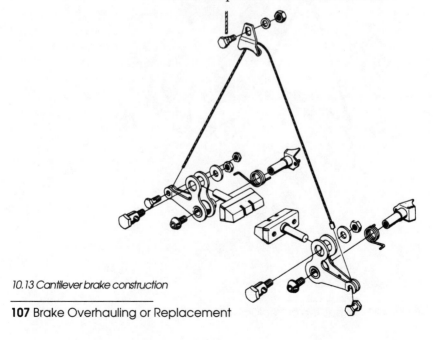

10.13 Cantilever brake construction

4. Using the needle-nose pliers, remove the upper end of the spring of each brake arm from its seating, then pull the brake arm, the spring and the bushing off the pivot stud.

5. Clean, inspect and if necessary repair or replace any damaged parts. In particular, remove any rust from the pivot stud of the pivot boss, then apply some grease to this location. On the roller-cam, disassemble the rollers from the brake arms, and install them again after inspection, cleaning and lubrication.

6. If appropriate, disassemble the brake pads and their fixing bolts, in order to clean and if necessary replace them (if the brake pads are badly worn). Reinstall, following the instructions in the adjusting procedures for the brake in question or those under *Replacing Brake Pads*.

Installation procedure:

1. After ascertaining that all parts are functional, clean and, where appropriate, lightly greased, first put the springs on the pivot

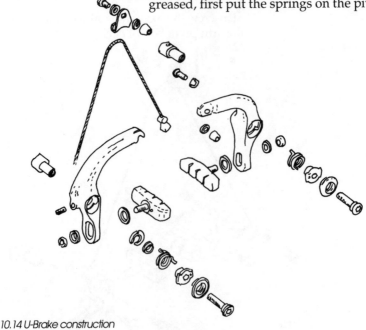

10.14 U-Brake construction

studs, with the long arms of the spring pointing up and to the inside.

2. Install the adjusting bushing over the top of the spring around the stud of each mounting boss, the cylindrical bushing part protruding.

3. Install the brake arms on the adjusting bushings, followed by the washer and the nut or the bolt.

4. In the case of a roller-cam brake, hook the end of the spring into its seating at the end of the roller pin of each brake arm.

5. Push the brake shoes together and reinstall the cam plate between the rollers (on the roller-cam) or the connecting cable (on other models). If appropriate, readjust the cable tension by adjusting at the brake lever or — if the deviation is significant — by clamping the anchor plate (U-brake or cantilever brake) or the cam plate (roller-cam brake) at a different point on the cable.

6. Carry out the adjustments outlined in the adjusting instruction for the particular brake.

Adjusting Brake Lever

Although there are a number of different makes and models, even within the category of specific mountain bike brake levers, the similarities are generally so great that the following general description covers all but the most unusual models. All are designed to fit standard 22.2 mm (7⁄8 in.) diameter handlebars as used on all regular mountain bikes. Any bike with a different diameter handlebar also requires a special clamp for the brake lever.

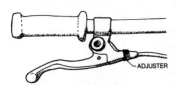

10.15 Brake cable adjuster

The brake lever must be installed so that it can be easily reached and pulled in so far, that the brake is fully applied when about 20 mm (3⁄4 in.) remains between the brake lever and the handlebars at the tightest point. Thus, there are three forms of adjustment of the brake lever:

☐ mounting location

☐ reach

☐ cable tension

Tools and equipment:
often Allen key, sometimes
open-ended wrench

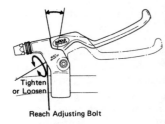

Reach Adjusting Bolt

*10.16 Brake lever reach
adjustment*

Procedure — location adjustment:
1. Determine in which direction, or directions, the brake lever should be moved or rotated to provide adequate and comfortable operation.

2. Establish whether any other parts installed on the handlebars (e.g. shift levers) may have to be moved in order to allow moving the brake lever to the desired location. Loosen these parts, so they can be easily moved.

3. Loosen the Allen key of the clamp that holds the lever to the handlebars by one or two turns, then twist or slide the lever in its desired location and tighten the clamping bolt again. Whatever you do, make sure the lever does not extend beyond the end of the handlebars, to avoid accidental brake application while passing closely by any objects in your path behind which the brake levers might get caught.

4. Retighten any other components that may have been moved to new locations; make sure all parts are in their most convenient location and are properly tightened.

Procedure — reach adjustment:
1. Most (though not all) mountain bike brake levers are equipped with a set screw such as the one shown in Fig. 10.16. This screw can be turned in or out in order to limit the range of travel of the brake lever as appropriate to the reach of your hand.

2. Check the distance between the handlebars and the brake lever in released position compared to the maximum comfortable reach of your hand. In generally, it should be opened as far as possible commensurate with the size of your hand, since a larger reach allows the most effective brake application and the most accurate adjustment of the brake cable.

3. If adjustment is necessary, tighten the range adjusting screw to reduce the range (i.e. the maximum opening position), or loosen it to increase the range.

4. Check to make sure the brake can be applied properly, and adjust the brake cable, following the appropriate instruction below, if necessary.

Adjusting Brake Cable

The main brake adjustment — the only one usually required from time to time to compensate for brake pad wear — is that of the brake cable. To adjust the brake cable tension, the lever is equipped with a barrel adjuster as shown in Fig. 10.17. In case the adjusting range of this device is not adequate, the attachment of the cable to the brake itself can be changed. The latter adjustment depends on the type of brake used, but can be generalized enough to cover most situations, as is done in the instructions below.

Tools and equipment:
often wrench and pliers

Procedure:
1. If the brake does not apply adequate force when the lever is pulled, the cable must be tightened. If, on the other hand, the brake seems to be applied too soon — e.g. when the brake scrapes the side of the rim when the lever is not pulled — it should be slackened a little.

2. To tighten the brake cable, hold the locknut and screw the barrel adjuster out by several turns. Then hold the barrel adjuster in place, while screwing in the locknut.

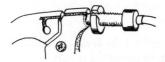

10.17 Brake cable with nipple in place showing slotted adjuster

3. To release the brake cable, hold the barrel adjuster and back off the locknut by several turns, then turn the barrel adjuster in further and turn the locknut in, holding the barrel adjuster to stop it from turning.

4. Check and readjust, if necessary, until operation of the brake is optimal.

5. If the adjusting range of the barrel adjuster is not adequate, screw it in all the way, after having backed off the locknut fully. Then proceed to adjust the clamping position of the cable at the brake.

6. The end of the cable at the brake unit itself is clamped onto an anchor by means of either an eye bolt or a pinch plate held under a bolt-

and-nut combination. Loosen the nut of this unit and pull the cable through a little further, then clamp it in properly at the new location by tightening the nut and countering the bolt.

7. Check once more and adjust the barrel adjuster at the brake lever if necessary.

Replacing Brake Cable

This should be done about once a year — or whenever it is pinched, corroded or otherwise damaged, especially if signs of broken strands, as shown in Fig. 10.18, are in evidence. Make sure you get a model that has the same kind of nipple (visible inside the lever) as the old one.

Tools and equipment:
wrench to fit cable clamp bolt, cable cutters, vaseline, possibly soldering equipment

Removal procedure:
1.   Release tension on the brake by squeezing the brake arms against the rim, then unhook the connecting cable (U-brake or cantilever brake) or the cam plate (roller-cam brake).

2.   Unscrew the eye bolt or clamp nut that holds the cable to the connecting plate, the cam plate or the brake itself (depending on the type of brake), making sure not to lose the various parts.

3.   Push the cable through towards the lever, then pull it out once enough slack is generated, catching any pieces of cable casing and end pieces.

4.   Screw the adjuster and the locknut at the lever in and leave them in such a position that their slots are aligned with the slot in the lever housing, so the cable can be lifted out.

5.   Remove the cable, dislodging the nipple

10.18 Broken cable strands

from the lever.

Installation procedure:
1.   Establish whether the cable casing is still intact and replace it if necessary, cutting it to length in such a way that no hook is formed at the end (bending the metal of the spiral back if necessary).

2.   Lubricate the inner cable with grease or vaseline.

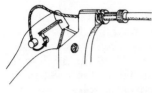

10.19 Cable nipple in brake lever

3. Place the nipple in the lever (Fig. 10.19) and guide the cable through the slot in the lever, the various guides and stops, and the sections of casing.

4. Attach the end in the eye bolt or clamp nut at the brake.

5. Adjust the cable tension as described above.

6. If you have the equipment to do it, solder the strands of the inner cable together before you cut it off, leaving about 2.5 cm (1 in.) projecting beyond the point where it will be clamped in.

7. Cut off the excess cable length. This is best done with a special cable cutting tool, though it can be done with other sharp and strong pliers, such as diagonal cutters. If you did not solder the ends together, install a cable end cap, and crimp it on with pliers.

Chapter 11
Accessories

Although, at least in the US, mountain bikes are generally ridden with no more than the essential equipment, several accessories have been introduced. This chapter will briefly describe how to install and maintain the most useful ones of these. We'll cover the following:

☐ lock

☐ pump

☐ seat adjuster (Hite-Rite)

☐ toeclips

☐ lights

☐ racks (luggage carriers)

☐ fenders (mudguards)

☐ chainring protector (Rockring).

The Lock

In most western societies this is unfortunately the most essential accessory. I suggest always carrying one, even off-road, and locking the machine whenever you leave it unguarded. Toughest to crack are the large reptile-like chains with cylindrical shackles, followed by U-shaped locks such as the Kryptonite. Another alternative is a heavy-duty plastic-coated cable with a separate lock, which should have a case-hardened shackle of 7.5 mm (5/16 in.) diameter to resist most common bike-theft equipment.

Lock Installation

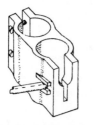

11.1 U-lock mounting bracket

The U-lock is easily mounted on the frame by means of a bracket supplied by the lock manufacturer (Fig. 11.1). Since mountain bike frame tubes may differ in diameters from those of other bikes, and since these locks come in different versions, make sure you take both bike and lock to the shop when selecting the bracket. If the bracket is loose on the tube or the lock, wrap one or more layers of handlebar tape (as used on ten-speeds) around the a frame tube. Install the bracket so that it does not interfere with access to the water bottle.

The cable lock is most easily carried in a bag hung off the saddle, though some models can be coiled up conveniently to hang behind the saddle. In that case, attach a strap on the back of the saddle to tie the cable down so it does not sway too much

Lock Maintenance

Lock maintenance is limited to cleaning and lubrication.

Tools and equipment:
thin mineral oil, rag

Lubricate the lock very sparingly after it has been cleaned: one or two drops of oil at the point where the shackle goes into the body of the lock, and one drop on the key — then insert the key to lock and unlock the thing a few times. Finally wipe off any excess lubricant.

The Pump

11.2 Pump head detail

At home, a big stand pump with hose connector is useful. On the bike, a smaller model will be needed. There are special mountain bike pumps available, in addition to regular bicycle pumps. The former have a larger diameter than the models intended for other bikes, allowing you to pump more air, though at a slightly lower pressure.

These pumps are also available to fit either directly between the frame tubes, between brazed or welded-on pegs, or between one peg and one of the tubes. A good place is behind the seat tube, if the frame's rear wheel clearance is adequate. Get a pump with the kind of head to match the valves on your bike's tires (Schrader or Presta, see Chapter 7). Recently, inflators with CO_2 have become popular. They are useful in a race, but for other purposes their time and weight savings features are not really worth the risk of 'running out of air' (CO_2 to be precise).

Pump Maintenance

If the pump doesn't work properly, the leak is usually at the head of the pump (the part that

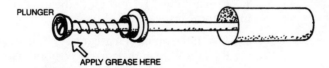

11.3 Pump maintenance detail

is put on the valve) or at the plunger inside the pump.

Tools and equipment:
wrench, lubricant

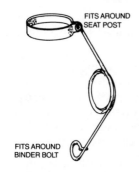

11.4 Hite-Rite seat adjuster

Seat Adjuster (Hite-Rite)

Replacing or Installing Hite-Rite

Tools and Equipment:
wrench, screwdriver

Procedure:
1.   Tighten the screwed bushing that holds down the grommet, or rubber sealing washer, in the head of the pump (Fig. 11.2).

2.   If this doesn't solve the problem, unscrew it and check the grommet (Fig. 11.3), replacing it if necessary (inflexible, cut, frayed or enlarged hole); then screw the bushing back on.

3.   If still no luck, unscrew the other end of the pump and check the condition of the leather or plastic plunger (Fig. 11.3). If it is no longer flexible, impregnate it with any kind of vegetable or animal fat and make sure it is screwed down tight. If necessary, replace the leather or plastic plunger.

The Hite-Rite, shown in Fig. 11.4, is a useful device, not only to adjust your seat while riding the bike, but also because it prevents saddle theft (or vandalism) and because it always keeps the saddle perfectly aligned after you have adjusted its height.

Once installed, you will rarely have to remove a Hite-Rite, though you may want to be able to do it — or install one later. Here's how it's done.

Removal procedure:
1.   Loosen the clamp that holds it around the seatpost.

2.   Remove the saddle with the seatpost as described in Chapter 6.

3.   Remove the quick-release binder bolt by unscrewing the thumbnut all the way.

4.   Pull the Hite-Rite off the seat lug's eye bolt.

Installation procedure:
1.   Consult Fig. 11.4 and place the lower clip in position at the seat lug's eye bolt.

2.   Install the quick-release binder bolt, holding the Hite-Rite in the correct position with the eye between the seat lug eye and the thumbnut

3. Loosely install the seatpost with the saddle as described in Chapter 6.

4. Tighten the Hite-Rite clamp around the seatpost when the seat is at the highest point you'll ever want it to be.

5. Complete installation and adjustment of the seatpost and the saddle as described in Chapter 6.

6. Check to make sure the seatpost can be adjusted over the desired range and make any corrections necessary.

Toeclips

11.5 Strapless toeclip

Nowadays, many mountain bikes are equipped with special toeclips. In addition to those similar to the ones used for ten-speed bikes that are strapped around the shoe, there are plastic devices as shown in Fig. 11.5 as well as simple heavy-duty straps. The latter two types merely act to stop the foot from slipping off the pedal, without locking it in there completely. Like the other type, they are installed on the pedal with a set of small screws with nuts to lock them in place. Just make sure they are put on pointing forward (the holes on the other side of the pedal are intended to install pedal reflectors).

Lights

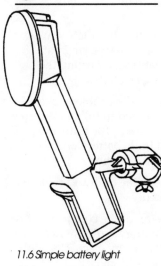

11.6 Simple battery light

For nighttime riding under off-road conditions, no single light seems to be bright enough. A full moon will serve you much better than most of these. However, for cycling on roads and reasonably surfaced paths, adequate lighting is available — and essential if you ride at night, since any encounter with pedestrians and other bikers could be fatal if both are unlit.

Only battery lights seem to be suitable, and I suggest you look for the biggest and brightest you can find. The light should throw a relatively wide beam, easily compared by shining several lights straight ahead at a light wall from the same distance. So many different varieties exist, that precise instructions are elusive. The following hints should be observed though.

Although brighter lights can be obtained with separate rechargeable battery units, the simplest acceptable lights are powered by at least two D-cells (the large cylindrical ones) each. Amongst those, the best reasonably priced ones seem to be the British Ever-Readies (known as Berec and Chloride in some countries), illustrated in Fig. 11.6.

Installing Lights

This has to be very general advice, since there are so many makes and models, all differing in detail.

Tools and equipment:
varies from make to make

Get the appropriate mounting hardware and install the lights in such a way that they do not protrude beyond the bike more than necessary. The highest mounting position is generally the best, since it throws less confusing shadows and is more readily visible to others.

Most popular amongst rear lights these days is the flashing LED type such as the Vista Light. Instead of a battery-powered rear light, a really big reflector, mounted rather low, is equally visible to all who have lighting themselves and could endanger you from behind. Amber is more visible than red, so should be preferred wherever the law does not prohibit its use (oddly enough, many states require rear lights and reflectors to be red).

Light Maintenance

This too has to be very general advice, but universally valid for all battery systems.

Tools and equipment:
spare batteries, spare bulb, sandpaper, battery terminal grease

Procedure:
1.   Usually, when a battery light lets you down, it's a matter of a dead or dying battery. Always check that first, by trying the light with other batteries installed.

2.   If that does not solve the problem, check whether the bulb is screwed in fully and contacts the terminal — screw in the bulb and scrape the contacts of bulb, battery and terminal to remove dirt or corrosion.

3.   If still no luck, check the bulb and replace it if the filament is broken.

4.   To prevent corrosion of the contacts, lightly coat the terminals of battery, bulb, switch and any other parts that carry electricity with battery terminal grease.

On lighting systems with rechargeable batteries and wiring connections, occasionally
check the connections and recharge the
NiCad batteries used at least once a week,
since these things have a limited shelf life, i.e.
they drain when not in use.

Luggage Racks

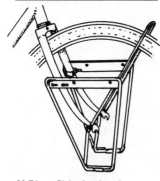

11.7 Low-Rider front rack

Special racks, luggage carriers to my British
readers, designed for the mountain bike's
generous dimensions, are readily available.
The granddaddy of all modern racks is Jim
Blackburn's welded aluminum model, and this
is still the declared favorite of many riders,
even if the competition offers significantly
cheaper racks that look quite similar.

In the front, use only the so-called Low-Rider
variety, illustrated in Fig. 11.7. These allow luggage to be carried where it least interferes with
steering and bike handling — centered on the
steering axis, just behind the front wheel axle.
Unfortunately, they do make it hard to
transport the bike on most car roof racks.

Luggage Rack
Installation

11.8 Patch to install clip

Generally, all luggage racks are attached to
bosses welded or brazed onto the bike's frame
and front fork.

If your bike does not have the requisite bosses,
a clip can be used, providing you first wrap the
frame or fork tube local to this clip with a large
rubber patch, installed with rubber solution
just like you would do for a flat tire, as illustrated in Fig. 11.8. This protects the paint
and prevents slipping of the clip under the
effect of load and vibrations.

Fenders

Fenders, referred to as mudguards in Britain,
are shown in Fig. 11.9. They are not generally
used on mountain bikes in the U.S. However,
if you ride in rainy weather or merely on wet
roads or trails, they are essential. Several
models are available, the widest and the
longest ones being the most effective. Short
clip-on guards don't usually do the trick. In
very heavy mud, especially on modern
American mountain bikes with their limited
wheel clearances, fenders can be more hassle
than they are worth, since the mud builds up

Installing Fenders

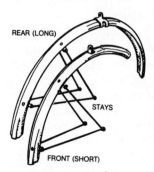

11.9 Fenders (mudguards)

*11.10 Home-made
quick-mounting bolt*

Chainring Protector
(Rockring)

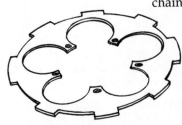

*11.11 Rockring chainring
protector.*

Other Accessories

between wheel and fender, soon rendering the former nearly immobile.

The stays with which the fenders are attached to the eyelets at the dropouts and the clips are attached by a bolt through a hole in the fork crown or in the bridge connecting the seat stays in the back. If your bike is lacking one or even both of these holes, it's possible to drill your own. If you want to make the fenders easily removable, use home-made wing-bolts, made by soldering a washer in the (widened) saw cut of a slotted-head screw, as illustrated in Fig. 11.10.

To straighten out the position of the fenders, the stays are merely clamped in at a different point. Cut off the excess length, so there are no dangerous protrusions on the bike. In fact, CPSC rules that only apply to children's bicycles sold in the US (but are often enforced on adult bikes as well) require a form of mounting by which the stays are inside the attachment. On these, the stays must be cut to the right length first.

This device, shown in Fig. 11.11, is a useful accessory for riding in rough terrain, especially over rocks and logs. It serves to protect the chainrings from damage. The Rockring is installed in the same holes as the chainrings, so make sure you get the right version to match your equipment. Use the special (longer) mounting bolts provided. It is of course also possible to install a strong metal guard directly on the bike, instead of on the chainrings, as a few international manufacturers do. Check the attachment from time to time, and tighten the bolts if necessary.

In addition to those items described in some details above, numerous other accessories are available, ranging from carrying straps and shoulder pads to derailleur protectors and brake covers, all specially designed with the mountain bike in mind. And then there are the many more or less useful accessories for general bicycle use.

What amongst all these gadgets will be useful is up to you to decide. My preference is to adorn my bike as little as possible, while some others I know buy every new gizmo that hits the market. Only too often, these items are never installed — or, if they are, soon removed again.

Notwithstanding some honorable exceptions that prove more practical than they seemed at first, the problem only too often is that many of these items have not been designed by experienced mountain bike riders, or if they are, they often have not been adequately tested in practical use first.

Not to discourage you, some items may well prove useful for one cyclist or the other. So install what appeals to you. Just keep the basic principles of part attachment and maintenance that are listed below in mind.

Accessory Installation and Maintenance

☐ Attachment must be at a minimum of two points, preferably off-set relative to one another.

☐ If it comes loose, don't just retighten it, but find a better attachment method.

☐ If it gets damaged, remove, repair or replace it immediately.

☐ If it is a moving part, check whether it moves freely without resistance, and lubricate or adjust it if necessary.

Back Matter

Troubleshooting Guide

Problem or Symptom	Possible Cause	Required Correction	See Page
Tiring riding position	1. Incorrect saddle adjustment	Adjust saddle	52–53
	2. Incorrect handlebar adjustment	Adjust handlebars	43
	3. Incorrect stem extension	Replace stem	45
	4. Incorrect frame size	Replace bike or frame	N/A
High resistance while coasting or pedaling	1. Tire rubs on frame or accessory	Adjust or straighten wheel	57–59
	2. Hub bearings worn or tight	Adjust and lubricate	61–62
	3. Insufficient tire pressure	Inflate tire	31, 66
High resistance while pedaling only	1. Chain dirty, worn or dry	Clean, lubricate, or replace	81–82
	2. Bottom bracket bearings out of adjustment	Adjust, lubricate, overhaul, or replace	73–74
	3. Pedal bearings out of adjustment	Adjust, lubricate, or replace	79–80
	4. Chain or chainring rubs on frame	Straighten or replace, correct chain line	81–82, 77–78
Rubbing or scraping sounds while pedaling or coasting	1. See above (as for *High resistance when pedaling*)	See above	
Bike pulls to one side	1. Wheels misaligned	Adjust, center, and align	57–59, 64
	2. Front fork bent	Replace or straighten	49–50
	3. Headset damaged	Overhaul or replace	47–48
	4. Frame out of alignment	Straighten or replace	38–40

Problem	Cause	Solution	Page
Bike vibrates at high speed	1. Wheels misaligned	Adjust or align	57–59, 64
	2. Hub bearings loose	Adjust	61–62
	3. Headset out of adjustment	Adjust, overhaul, or replace	47–48
Disturbing noises while pedaling	1. Chainring, crank or pedal loose	Fasten or replace	75–81
	2. Chain dry, dirty or worn	Clean, lubricate, or replace	82–83
	3. Bottom bracket bearing or pedal bearing out of adjustment	Adjust, lubricate, overhaul	73–74, 79–80
Chain jumps or skips	1. New chain on worn sprocket	Replace sprocket or entire freewheel	85–88
	2. Chain worn or slack	Replace chain	81–82
	3. Stiff or bent chain link	Replace link or chain	81–82
Chain drops off chainwheel or sprocket	1. Derailleur out of adjustment	Adjust derailleurs	90–92, 95
	2. Chainring bent or loose	Straighten or tighten	78
	3. Incorrect chain line	Correct chain line	81–83
Irregular pedaling movement	1. Crank, bottom bracket or pedal loose	Adjust or tighten	73–80
	2. Pedal spindle or crank bent	Replace	80
Rubbing noise while pedaling	1. Wrong gear selected	Avoid cross-chain	89–90
	2. Front derailleur out of adjustment	Adjust front derailleur	95
	3. Front derailleur under angle	Reposition front derailleur	96

Problem or Symptom	Possible Cause	Required Correction	See Page
Gears do not engage properly	1. Derailleur out of adjustment	Adjust derailleur	92, 95
	2. Derailleur dirty or damaged	Overhaul derailleur	94
	3. Shift lever or cable damaged, corroded or maladjusted	Clean, lubricate, adjust, or replace	97, 98
	4. Chain too short or too long	Correct or replace	82
	5. Front derailleur loose or not straight	Tighten and align	96
	6. Cable damaged or corroded	Replace and lubricate	98
	7. Chain or sprockets worn	Replace	82, 87–88
Brake ineffective	1. Brake out of adjustment	Adjust brake	102
	2. Brake pads worn	Replace	102
	3. Rim wet, greasy or dirty	Clean rim	34
	4. Brake cable corroded, pinched or damaged	Free, lubricate or replace cable	26, 111–112
	5. Brake lever loose or damaged	Tighten, free, lubricate, or replace lever	109
	6. Wheel seriously out of round	Straighten rim	64–55
	7. Brake loose or bent	Tighten, free, lubricate, or replace	106
Brake jitters	1. Brake loose	Tighten mounting bolt	106
	2. Rim seriously out of round	Straighten rim	64–65
	3. Rim dirty or greasy	Clean rim	34
	4. Headset loose	Adjust headset	47

Problem	Cause	Remedy	Page
Brake squeals	1. Brake pads contact rim poorly	Adjust or bend brake arm	102
	2. Rim dirty	Clean rim	34
	3. Brake pads worn or dirty	Replace brake pads	102
	4. Brake arms loose	Tighten pivot bolt	106
Conventional battery lighting defective	1. Battery exhausted	Replace battery	118
	2. Battery contact defective	Clean, bend, scrape	118
	3. Contact in lamp housing defective	Repair contact	118
	4. Switch defective	Clean contacts, bend spring	118
	5. Bulb loose or defective	Reseat or replace bulb	118
Rechargeable battery lighting defective	1. Battery exhausted	Recharge or replace battery	118
	2. Battery contact defective	Clean, bend, scrape	118
	3. Wiring contact loose	Repair connection	118
	4. Contact in lamp housing defective	Repair contact	118
	5. Switch defective	Clean contacts, bend spring	118
	6. Bulb loose or defective	Reseat or replace bulb	118

Index

A
accessories, 15, 114–121
adjustable bearing, 28
adjustable spanner, (see crescent wrench)
Allen key, 18
AHeadSet, 51
axle nut, 59

B
ball bearings, 28
bar ends, 47
ball bearings, 28
   adjustment, 29
bi-weekly inspection, 32
bike stand, 30
binder bolt, 52
bottom bracket, 73
   adjustment, 74
   overhaul, 74
   tools, 21,74
Bowden cable, 26
box wrench, 17
brake, 14, 100"113
   adjustment, 102
   overhaul, 107
   replacement, 107
   types, 100
brake cable, 111
brake lever, 109
BSA bottom bracket, 73
buckled wheel, 65

C
cable, 27
   adjuster, 26
   nipple, 26
cantilever brake, 100
   centering, 103
cartridge bearing, 28
   bottom bracket, 73
cassette freewheel, 87–88
cassette hub, 84
centering brake, 103
chain, 82
   lubrication, 82
   replacement,82
chain lubricant, 21
chain rivet tool, 20
chain whip, 20

chainring, 77
   attachment, 78
   damage, 78
chainring protector, 120
cleaning, 35
   materials, 21
clipless pedals, 81
CO2 inflator, 115
cogs (see sprockets)
components, 13–14
cone wrench, 20
crank, 75
   attachment, 75
   extractor, 20
   replacement, 76
crank tool (see crank extractor)
crescent wrench, 17

D
daily inspection, 32
derailleur, 14, 89
   adjustment, 90
   overhaul, 94
   range, 90
double-wire (saddle) adaptor, 56
drivetrain, 14, 73
drop-out, 39
   alignment, 40

E
emergency spoke, 67
emergency tools, 17, 22

F
fender installation, 120
file, 18
flat (see puncture)
fork, also see front fork), 50
   replacement, 50
frame, 13, 36
   alignment, 38
   components, 36
   construction, 36
   damage, 37
   materials, 37
   tubes, 13, 36
freewheel, 84

lubrication, 85
   replacement, 85
front derailleur, 95–96
   adjustment, 96
   replacement, 96
front fork, 50
functional systems, 13

G
gear cable, 27, 98
gearing system, 14, 89
grease, 21

H
hammer, 18
handgrips, 46
handlebars, 42
   adjustment, 43
   installation, 44
   replacement, 44
   width, 46
handlebar stem (see stem)
headset, 47
   adjustment, 47
   overhauling, 48
headset tools, 21
Hite-Rite, 116
   replacement and installation, 116
hubs, 57, 60
   adjustment, 60
   maintenance, 60
   overhaul, 63
hub bearings, 61
Hyperglide chain, 82, 84

I
improvised tools, 19
indexed gearing, 90

L
leather saddle, 55
left-hand (LH) screw thread, 24
lights, 117
   installation, 118
   maintenance, 118
lock, 114
   installation, 114

lock (continued)
 maintenance, 115
low-profile brakes, 101, 103
lubricants, 21
lubrication, 33
luggage carrier (see rack)

M
mallet, 18
methodology, 11
mudguards (see fenders)

N
nipple (for spoke), 64
nipple spanner (see spoke wrench)
non-indexed derailleur, 94

O
oil, 21
open-ended wrench, 18

P
paint, 40
 damage, 40
 touching up, 40
pedal, 78
 adjustment, 80
 maintenance, 80
 overhaul, 80
 replacement, 78
 threading, 78
penetrating oil, 21
pliers, 18
preventive maintenance, 31–33
pump, 19, 115
 maintenance, 115
puncture, 67

Q
quality of tools, 16
quick-release, 28
 binder bolt, 52
 hub, 57

R
rack, 119
 rear derailleur, 91
 adjustment, 92
 overhaul, 94
 replacement, 94
rear triangle alignment, 38
rim, 64
Rockring, 120
roller-cam brake, 100, 104
 adjustment, 104

S
saddle, 14, 52
 adjustment, 52–53
 maintenance, 55
 position, 53
saw, 18
screw thread, 24
screwdriver, 17
sealed bearing (see cartridge bearing)
seat (see saddle)
seatpost, 14, 52
semi-annual inspection, 33
shifter, 14, 97
 maintenance, 98
 replacement, 97
solvent, 21
spanners (see wrenches)
spare parts, 23
specific bicycle tools, 17–19
spelling, 11
spoke, 64

emergency, 67
 replacement, 66
spoke wrench, 20
sprocket, 84
 replacement, 86
steering system, 13, 42
stem, 44
suspension, 15, 51

T
terminology, 11
thumb shifter, 97
tire (and tube), 67
 dimensions, 67
 repair, 68, 71
 replacement, 71
tire lever, 20
tire repair kit, 20
toeclip, 117
 installation, 117
tools, 16–22
touch-up paint, 40
tube (see tube)
twistgrip shifter, 99

U
U-brake, 100
 centering, 104
under-the-bar shifter, 89
unicrown fork, 50
universal tools, 16–17

V
valve, 57, 67

W
wheel, 14, 57
 components, 57
 replacement, 57, 59
 truing, 64
wishbone shifter, 97
workshop, 30
workshop procedure, 24

Other Titles Available from Bicycle Books

Title	Author	US Price
All Terrain Biking	Jim Zarka	$7.95
The Backroads of Holland	Helen Colijn	$12.95
The Bicycle Commuting Book	Rob van der Plas	$7.95
The Bicycle Fitness Book	Rob van der Plas	$7.95
The Bicycle Repair Book	Rob van der Plas	$9.95
Bicycle Technology	Rob van der Plas	$16.95
Bicycle Touring International	Kameel Nasr	$18.95
The Bicycle Touring Manual	Rob van der Plas	$16.95
Bicycling Fuel	Richard Rafoth	$9.95
Cycling Europe	Nadine Slavinski	$12.95
Cycling France	Jerry Simpson	$12.95
Cycling Kenya	Kathleen Bennett	$12.95
Cycling the San Francisco Bay Area	Carol O'Hare	$12.95
Cycling the U.S. Parks	Jim Clark	$12.95
In High Gear (hardcover)	Samuel Abt	$21.95
In High Gear (paperback)	Samuel Abt	$10.95
The High Performance Heart	Maffetone & Mantell	$9.95
Major Taylor (hardcover)	Andrew Ritchie	$19.95
The Mountain Bike Book	Rob van der Plas	$10.95
Mountain Bike Magic (color)	Rob van der Plas	$14.95
Mountain Bike Maintenance	Rob van der Plas	$9.95
Mountain Bikes: Maint. & Repair*	John Stevenson	$22.50
Mountain Bike Racing (hardcover)*	Burney & Gould	$22.50
The New Bike Book	Jim Langley	$4.95
Roadside Bicycle Repairs	Rob van der Plas	$4.95
Tour of the Forest Bike Race (color)	H. E. Thomson	$9.95
Tour de France (hardcover)	Samuel Abt	$22.95
Tour de France (paperback)	Samuel Abt	$12.95

Buy our books at your local book shop or bike store.

Book shops can obtain these titles for you from our book trade distributor (National Book Network for the USA), bike shops directly from us. If you have difficulty obtaining our books elsewhere, we will be pleased to supply them by mail, but we must add $2.50 postage and handling (and California Sales Tax if mailed to a California address). Prepayment by check (or credit card information) must be included with your order.

Bicycle Books, Inc.
PO Box 2038
Mill Valley CA 94941
Tel.: (415) 381-0172

In Britain: Bicycle Books
463 Ashley Road
Poole, Dorset BH14 0AX
Tel.: (0202) 71 53 49

---

* Books marked thus not available from Bicycle Books in the U.K.
